Beyond the Rope

Beyond the Rope is an interdisciplinary study that draws on narrative theory and cultural studies methodologies to trace African Americans' changing attitudes and relationships to lynching over the twentieth century. Whereas African Americans are typically framed as victims of white lynch mob violence in both scholarly and public discourses, Karlos K. Hill reveals that in the late nineteenth and early twentieth centuries, African Americans lynched other African Americans in response to alleged criminality, and twentieth-century black writers envisaged African American lynch victims as exemplars of heroic manhood. *Beyond the Rope* illuminates the submerged histories of black vigilantism and black-authored narratives of the lynched black body in order to demonstrate that, rather than being static and one-dimensional, African American attitudes toward lynching and the lynched black evolved in response to changing social and political contexts.

Dr. Karlos K. Hill is Associate Professor of History at Texas Tech University.

Cambridge Studies on the American South

Series Editors

Mark M. Smith, University of South Carolina, Columbia
David Moltke-Hansen, Center for the Study of the American South, University of North Carolina at Chapel Hill

Interdisciplinary in its scope and intent, this series builds on and extends Cambridge University Press's long-standing commitment to studies on the American South. The series not only offers the best new work on the South's distinctive institutional, social, economic, and cultural history but also features works with a national, comparative, and transnational perspective.

Titles in the Series

Robert E. Bonner, *Mastering America: Southern Slaveholders and the Crisis of American Nationhood*
Ras Michael Brown, *African-Atlantic Cultures and the South Carolina Lowcountry*
Christopher Michael Curtis, *Jefferson's Freeholders and the Politics of Ownership in the Old Dominion*
Louis A. Ferleger and John D. Metz, *Cultivating Success in the South: Farm Households in Postbellum Georgia*
Craig Friend and Lorri Glover, eds., *Death and the American South*
Luke E. Harlow, *Religion, Race, and the Making of Confederate Kentucky, 1830–1880*
Ari Helo, *Thomas Jefferson's Ethics and the Politics of Human Progress: The Morality of a Slaveholder*
Susanna Michele Lee, *Claiming the Union: Citizenship in the Post–Civil War South*
William A. Link and James J. Broomall, eds., *Rethinking American Emancipation: Legacies of Slavery and the Quest for Black Freedom*
Scott P. Marler, *The Merchants' Capital: New Orleans and the Political Economy of the Nineteenth-Century South*
Peter McCandless, *Slavery, Disease, and Suffering in the Southern Lowcountry*
James Van Horn Melton, *Religion, Community, and Slavery on the Colonial Southern Frontier*
Barton A. Myers, *Rebels against the Confederacy: North Carolina's Unionists*
Johanna Nicol Shields, *Freedom in a Slave Society: Stories from the Antebellum South*
Damian Alan Pargas, *Slavery and Forced Migration in the Antebellum South*
Brian Steele, *Thomas Jefferson and American Nationhood*
Jonathan Daniel Wells, *Women Writers and Journalists in the Nineteenth-Century South*

Beyond the Rope

The Impact of Lynching on Black Culture and Memory

KARLOS K. HILL
Texas Tech University

CAMBRIDGE
UNIVERSITY PRESS

University Printing House, Cambridge CB2 8BS, United Kingdom

One Liberty Plaza, 20th Floor, New York, NY 10006, USA

477 Williamstown Road, Port Melbourne, VIC 3207, Australia

4843/24, 2nd Floor, Ansari Road, Daryaganj, Delhi - 110002, India

79 Anson Road, #06-04/06, Singapore 079906

Cambridge University Press is part of the University of Cambridge.

It furthers the University's mission by disseminating knowledge in the pursuit of education, learning and research at the highest international levels of excellence.

www.cambridge.org
Information on this title: www.cambridge.org/9781107620377

First published 2016

A catalogue record for this publication is available from the British Library

ISBN 978-1-107-04413-5 Hardback
ISBN 978-1-107-62037-7 Paperback

Contents

Tables and Figures

TABLES

FIGURES

Acknowledgments

There are many people who contributed to making this book possible. For starters, no one could ask for better mentors than Peter Rachleff, James Stewart, Sundiata Cha-Jua, and David Roediger. Peter Rachleff and James Stewart inspired me to do professional history. During my undergraduate days when the thought of writing a graduate thesis seemed farfetched, both Rachleff and Stewart encouraged me to pursue a PhD in history. Unbeknownst to them, they were to be the foundation of my academic career. During graduate school, Sundiata Cha-Jua encouraged me to pursue the history of lynching as a dissertation topic. Since then, he has helped guide the book project and more importantly has modeled how to do research, writing, and teaching that matters. For this, I will always be grateful. David Roediger's support has been nothing short of angelic. Dave provided detailed feedback on the manuscript from beginning to end. His generosity is inspiring. He is truly a model of a mentor-colleague.

My colleagues and friends at Texas Tech University are wonderful. Aliza Wong and Gretchen Adams read early drafts of the book proposal. Even in the book's early stages, they spurred me on and helped me see the broader significance of the project. Aliza deserves particular praise in that her thoughtful feedback always nurtures one's creativity, and her boundless generosity uplifts the soul. In addition, colleagues Saad Abi-Hamad, Manu Vimalassery, Paul Bjerk, Emily Skidmore, Jacob Baum, Miguel Levario, Sean Cunningham, Zach Brittsan, Corby Kelly, and Maurice Hobson supported the project in indirect but nonetheless meaningful ways.

I hope I can return the favor someday. In the final stages of the book revision process, TTU's Competitive Arts, Humanities, and Social Sciences grant allowed me to take a semester of leave in order to finish the book. During this period, I was able to do some of my best thinking and writing.

The editors at Cambridge University Press are first-rate in every way. David Moltke-Hansen, Mark Smith, and Lou Bateman read and critiqued several versions of the book proposal. Their thoughtful and incisive criticism pushed the book project in new and productive directions. Deborah Gershenowitz's guidance of the project has humbled me. With her support and expertise, my initial manuscript has flowered into a book.

Finally, this book is dedicated to my family. In particular, without the unconditional support of my wife and partner, Jennie Hill, this book project would not have been possible. Through it all, she has modeled what it means to be a caring and supportive spouse.

Lubbock, Texas
August 2015

Introduction

James Allen, an Atlanta-based antiques collector, debuted *Witness: Photographs of Lynchings from the Collection of James Allen* at the Ruth Horowitz Gallery in Manhattan in January 2000. The exhibit displayed sixty photographs and postcards of lynchings that primarily depicted white-on-black lynch mob violence. It created an immediate buzz. People waited for hours in long lines to view the collection, which led the gallery to issue two hundred tickets per day. At least five thousand people viewed the exhibit before it closed. Subsequently, James Allen renamed the exhibit *Without Sanctuary* and redisplayed the photographs at the New York Historical Society between March 14 and October 1, 2000, during which time more than fifty thousand people viewed the collection. From there, it was exhibited in Pittsburg, Atlanta, and even at the Sorbonne in Paris. Altogether, between 2000 and 2009, *Without Sanctuary* was exhibited eight times. Even though Allen and museum curators modified or changed some aspects at each new site, the exhibition set attendance records for the host museums. Based upon the exhibit's popularity, Twin Palms Press published ninety-eight of Allen's lynching photos and postcards in *Without Sanctuary: Lynching Photography in America* in late 2000. Since publication, it has sold over sixty thousand copies. Thus, perhaps more than any other individual in the past two decades, James Allen has inserted the history of lynching into mainstream consciousness.

The *Without Sanctuary* exhibition and book showcase the most familiar images of American lynching – images of white lynchers surrounding a lynched black body. Contrary to the original intent of

FIGURE 1 Onlookers at the Jesse Washington Lynching. "Large crowd watching the lynching of Jesse Washington, 18- year-old African American, in Waco, Texas, May 15, 1916."
Source: Courtesy of the Library of Congress, Prints and Photographs Division; visual materials from the NAACP Records, lot 13093, no. 33.

FIGURE 2 Close-Up of Jesse Washington's Mutilated Body. "Charred corpse of Jesse Washington after lynching, Waco, Texas, May 15, 1916." *Source:* Courtesy of the Library of Congress, Prints and Photographs Division; visual materials from the NAACP Records, lot 13093, no. 35.

lynching photographs, *Without Sanctuary* employs these images for the purpose of perpetuating a victimization narrative of the lynched black body. This narrative hinges upon highlighting white brutality against blacks. Rhetorically, *Without Sanctuary* aims to elicit contemporary audiences' outrage, sympathy for black lynch victims and their families, and reprobation for whites who participated in, witnessed, and condoned these brutal murders. It is an important and necessary narrative that has its roots in the National Association of the Advancement of Colored People's (NAACP) four-decade quest for a federal antilynching law during the first half of the twentieth century. However, although the victimization narrative presented in *Without Sanctuary* is important and perhaps most familiar to contemporaries, it is in fact only one among many black-authored narratives that have chronicled lynching. In what follows, I will identify, describe, and historicize the victimization narrative as well as less familiar, but nonetheless significant, black-authored narratives of lynching.

Specifically, this book traces the evolution of black-authored narratives of the lynched black body from the 1880s to the 1990s by examining lynching narratives found in mainstream newspapers, the African American press, African American literature, and oral history interviews of African Americans. I define "lynching narratives" as both fictional and nonfictional stories in which lynching is central to the story's plot. In particular, this book illustrates how black Americans developed narratives of the lynched black body in response to the dramatic rise in white-on-black lynching and the emergence of the black beast rapist discourse in the late 1880s and early 1890s. *Beyond the Rope* emphasizes how black-authored lynching narratives sought to shape black attitudes toward the lynched black body. To be clear, the lynched black body is not employed here as a metaphor or some other abstraction. Rather, "the lynched black body" refers to actual flesh-and-blood or fictionalized black Americans who were executed by a lynch mob for an alleged offense. When lynched black bodies enter narrative discourse, they become a rhetorical instrument that attempts to convey specific meanings to specific audiences for specific purposes.[1]

[1] James Phelan, *Experiencing Fiction: Judgments, Progressions, and the Rhetorical Theory of Narrative* (Columbus: Ohio State University, 2007), 3. For frameworks for understanding rhetorical approaches to narrative, see Wayne C. Booth, *The Rhetoric of Fiction* (Chicago: University of Chicago Press, 1965); Wayne C. Booth, *The Company We Keep: An Ethics of Fiction* (Berkeley: University of

In tracing how narratives of the lynched black body changed over time, *Beyond the Rope* argues that the lynched black body in the black cultural imagination is best understood as a floating signifier that could be fashioned for varying rhetorical purposes, depending upon the circumstances of the times. Cultural theorist Stuart Hall employed the term "floating signifier" to explain how "there is nothing solid or permanent to the meaning of race." According to Hall, race is a floating signifier "because it is relational, and not essential, can never be finally fixed, but is subject to the constant process of redefinition and appropriation." Consequently, *race* can be "made to mean something different in different cultures, in different historical formations, at different moments of time."[2] Understanding the lynched black body as a floating signifier is important because it reveals that black perspectives toward black lynch victims have ranged from viewing black vigilantism against other African Americans as warranted to framing black victims of white lynch mob violence as hapless victims or the subjects of what I refer to as "victimization narratives" of the lynched black body. Alternatively, black Americans have portrayed black victims of white lynch mob violence as exemplars of heroic manhood in what I refer to more broadly as "consoling narratives" of the lynched black body. In bringing to light the various ways in which black Americans have portrayed black lynch victims in lynching narratives, my aim is to demonstrate that black attitudes toward the lynched black body have been fluid and contingent rather than one-dimensional and static.

In *Beyond the Rope*, I am not suggesting that victimization narratives or consoling narratives of the lynched black body

California Press, 1988); James Phelan, *Narrative as Rhetoric: Techniques, Audiences, Ethics, and Ideology* (Columbus: Ohio University Press, 1996); Arthur W. Frank, *Letting Stories Breathe: A Socio-narratology* (Chicago: University of Chicago Press, 2010); Hayden White, *Figural Realism: Studies in the Mimesis Effect* (Baltimore: Johns Hopkins University, 1999); Walter Fisher, "Narration, Knowledge, and the Possibility of Wisdom," in *Rethinking Knowledge: Reflections across the Disciplines*, eds. Robert F. Goodman and Walter Fisher (Albany: State University of New York Press, 1995); Jerome Bruner, "The Narrative Construction of Reality," *Critical Inquiry* 18 (1991): 1–21; and Hayden White, *The Content of the Form: Narrative Discourse and Historical Representation* (Baltimore: Johns Hopkins University, 1990).

[2] Stuart Hall, "Race, the Floating Signifier," https://www.mediaed.org/assets/products/407/transcript_407.pdf; see also Jeffery Mehlman, "The 'Floating Signifier': From Levi-Strauss to Lacan," *Yale French Studies* 48 (1972): 10–37.

necessarily reflect how black Americans thought about particular black lynch victims. Rather, I am arguing that black-authored lynching narratives reveal how black antilynching activists, black writers, and African Americans more broadly sought to construct a particular vision of black lynch victims for specific rhetorical purposes. For instance, while acknowledging that lynchings were painful, ugly stories, black Americans sought to make lynching narratives redemptive ones. Black writers such as Sutton Griggs and Richard Wright constructed lynching narratives in ways that highlighted black agency even though the ultimate outcome of these lynching narratives was the death of black bodies at the hands of white lynchers. More specifically, the redemptive power of consoling narratives of the lynched black body lies in the ability of these narratives to be an effective counterpoint to the humiliation and helplessness that the white supremacist version of the dehumanized lynched black body sought to inspire.

Beyond the Rope contributes to a small but growing list of histories that examine lynching and black cultural history. Since the late 1970s, histories of lynching have primarily focused on explaining why white-on-black lynching incidents skyrocketed at the turn of the twentieth century.[3] Because white perspectives were presumed to be most important in ascertaining why whites lynched blacks, black perspectives have garnered little critical examination. In the past five years, historians have become interested in black perspectives on lynching and specifically how and why blacks crafted counternarratives to white-on-black lynch mob violence. Representative works include Christopher Waldrep's *African Americans Confront Lynching* (2009), Leigh Raiford's *Imprisoned in a Luminous Glare* (2011), Koritha Mitchell's *Living with Lynching* (2011), Kidada E. Williams's *They Left Great Marks on Me* (2012), and Sandy Alexandre's *The Properties of Violence* (2012). This new scholarship on black perspectives and lynching is

[3] Representative works include Jacqueline Dowd Hall, *Revolt against Chivalry: Jesse Daniel Ames and the Women's Campaign against Lynching* (New York: Columbia University Press, 1979); W. Fitzhugh Brundage, *Lynching in the New South, Georgia and Virginia, 1880–1930* (Urbana: University of Illinois Press, 1993); Stewart Tolnay and E. M. Beck, *A Festival of Violence: An Analysis of Southern Lynchings, 1882–1930* (Urbana: University of Illinois Press, 1995); Michael J. Pfeifer, *Rough Justice: Lynching and American Society, 1874–1947* (Urbana: University of Illinois Press, 2006); Ashraf H. A. Rushdy, *American Lynching* (New Haven: Yale University Press, 2012).

the natural outgrowth of earlier scholarship on black resistance. For instance, during the late 1990s and early 2000s, historians began challenging the notion that black resistance to lynching did not occur during the era of Jim Crow by documenting black organized resistance to attempted lynchings or in response to a particular lynching.[4] Over time, historians interested in the relationship between lynching and black agency have gradually shifted from examining particular episodes of black resistance to lynching and more toward charting the black antilynching discourses that gave rise to such resistance.

Although the above-mentioned literature probes black perspectives on lynching by exploring a variety of primary sources from multiple vantage points, it exclusively examines black perspectives on lynching in relationship to white-on-black lynching. Yet African Americans were not only victims of vigilante violence during the late nineteenth and early twentieth centuries – they also participated in vigilante violence. In fact, between 1882 and 1930, Southern newspapers reported approximately 148 incidents in which black vigilantes lynched African Americans for alleged criminal activity. To be clear, "black vigilantism" refers to a lynching in which a group of African American vigilantes publicly executed another African American for an alleged offense. Despite extant newspaper documentation, the history of African Americans lynching other African Americans has been largely excised from official histories and historical memory. To date, few scholars have written article-length essays on the history of black vigilantism.[5] Collectively, these works explain the similarities and differences

[4] Representative works include W. Fitzhugh Brundage, "The Roar on the Other Side of Violence," in *Under Sentence of Death: Lynching in the South*, ed. W. Fitzhugh Brundage (Chapel Hill: University of North Carolina Press, 1997), 271–291, and Sundiata Cha-Jua, "'A Warlike Demonstration': Legalism, Violent Self-Help, and Electoral Politics in Decatur, Illinois, 1894–1898," *Journal of Urban History* 26, no. 5 (2000): 591–629.

[5] E. M. Beck and Stewart Tolnay, "When Race Didn't Matter: Black and White Mob Violence against Their Own Color," in *Under Sentence of Death: Lynching in the South*, ed. W. Fitzhugh Brundage (Chapel Hill: University of North Carolina Press, 1997); Bruce Baker, "Lynch Law Reversed: The Rape of Lula Sherman, the Lynching of Manse Waldrop, and the Debate over Lynching in the 1880s," *American Nineteenth Century History* 6 (2005); Karlos K. Hill, "Black Vigilantism: The Rise and Decline of African American Lynch Mob Activity in the Mississippi and Arkansas Deltas, 1883–1923," *Journal of African American History* 95 (2010).

between black vigilantism and white vigilantism from the 1880s to the 1930s. *Beyond the Rope* contends that the history of black vigilantism is foundational to understanding the black experience of lynching. By analyzing narratives of the lynched black body that developed in response to both black vigilantism and white-on-black vigilantism, *Beyond the Rope* will more fully map the historical trajectory of black Americans' perspectives toward black lynch victims.

I analyze lynching narratives created during the peak period of lynch mob violence in America (1880–1930) as well as those created during the 1990s, when lynching had ceased to be a social problem in America. This broad time frame is necessary in order to illustrate the arc of black Americans' perspectives on black lynch victims and particularly how black-authored lynching narratives were responsive to changing historical and rhetorical contexts. In addition, I examine mainstream newspapers, black newspapers, and black literature during the peak period of white-on-black lynch mob violence. Newspapers are crucial for scholarly examinations of lynching, because they provide the most accurate and detailed descriptions of particular lynchings. Also, because newspapers consistently contained lengthy editorials about lynching, they are useful sources with which to reconstruct societal attitudes on lynching. Black newspapers are a key source for reconstructing black perspectives on lynching; they were one of the primary conduits of black public opinion as well as a primary site for challenging antiblack rationales and representations of lynching typically found in mainstream newspapers. Besides newspapers, literature was a crucial genre for the construction and dissemination of lynching narratives. During the late nineteenth and early twentieth centuries, American literature was saturated with negative portrayals of black people, and especially of black lynch victims.[6] Unsurprisingly, many late nineteenth- and early twentieth-century African American literary works meditated on the problem of lynching and its impact on black life.[7] Therefore,

[6] For a discussion of seminal works in white supremacist fiction and lynching, see Sandra Gunning, *Race, Rape, and Lynching: The Red Record of American Literature, 1890–1912* (New York: Oxford University Press, 1996), especially chapter 1.

[7] For the best overview of African American writers and lynching, see Trudier Harris, *Exorcising Blackness: Historical and Literary Lynchings and Burning Rituals* (Bloomington: Indiana University Press, 1984), especially chapters 2–4.

African American literature provides a useful lens through which to reconstruct how black writers sought to create a counternarrative to racist justifications for lynching as well as reimagine the meaning of black lynch victims for black audiences. Lastly, I examine oral history interviews of African Americans compiled during the 1990s by the Behind the Veil Oral History Project – the largest and most comprehensive archive of African American interviews on black life in the Jim Crow South. I utilize oral history interviews in order to access the ideas and opinions of black Americans who did not or could not lodge their perspective in print culture. Moreover, since oral histories are constructed through weaving together both public and private memories, they provide an important lens for understanding how African Americans shaped a shared narrative of lynching long after lynching ceased to be a significant social problem for black Americans.

The critical context for this book is what I refer to as "the racialization of lynching": the process by which black Americans became the primary targets of white lynch mob violence. Although difficult to pinpoint, the period in which lynching became racialized occurred approximately between the years 1886 and 1892. In 1882, the *Chicago Tribune* – and eventually other mainstream newspapers – began tabulating the number of lynchings that occurred annually, the accusations that provoked them, and the racial identity of lynch victims. The year 1886 is important because it was the first time since lynching statistics began to be compiled that the total number of recorded black lynch victims exceeded the total number of recorded white lynch victims. In 1886, 74 blacks were lynched and 64 whites were lynched. After 1886, the total recorded number of white persons lynched never surpassed the total recorded number of black persons lynched. Moreover, the year 1892 bookends this period because 161 black lynchings occurred in that year – the most black lynchings recorded in a single year in American history. In that same year, there were 69 recorded white lynchings. Of the 1,075 recorded lynch victims between 1886 and 1892, blacks accounted for 780 (or 73 percent of total lynchings), whereas 295 whites were lynched (or 27 percent of total lynchings). The extent to which blacks had become the primary targets of lynch mob violence is made more apparent when one takes into consideration that between 1882 and 1885, blacks accounted for only 36 percent of total lynch victims and whites accounted for 64 percent of total lynch victims. Therefore, beginning in 1886 and continuing thereafter, lynch victims were typically black persons rather than white.[8]

In addition, the racialization of lynching refers to how the practice of lynching was increasingly justified in racially specific ways. As the number of black lynchings rose after 1886, racial rationalizations for lynching – and particularly the black beast rapist narrative – became prevalent. The black beast rapist narrative posited that since emancipation, black males had regressed to a primitive, bestial state. As a result, black males, unable to control their sexual lust and unrestrained by the moderating influence of slavery, began raping white women in alarming numbers. In both the North and South, white politicians and the white press trumpeted the story that, given heightened black male sexual aggression toward white women, lynching was necessary to deter black rapists. The black male rapist narrative represented an "emotional logic of lynching," which meant that only swift and sure violence unhampered by legalities could protect white women from sexual assault by black men.[9] By 1889, the association between black men and rape had become so thoroughly fused in the white imagination that many whites perceived the rape of white women as the "negro's crime."[10] In an 1894 speech entitled "Lessons of the Hour," Fredrick Douglass, the nation's foremost black spokesman, declared of this narrative, "It clouds the character of the negro with a crime most revolting, and is fitted to drive from him all sympathy and all fair play and mercy."[11] In sum, the racialization of lynching transformed lynching, which had been an extralegal form of social control, into a mechanism primarily for racial social control.

The racialization of lynching was linked to a broader political transformation in American society during the 1880s that aimed

[8] For the lynching statistics cited in this paragraph, see Robert Zangrando, *The NAACP Crusade against Lynching, 1909–1950* (Philadelphia: Temple University Press, 1980), 5–6.

[9] Jacqueline Dowd Hall, "'The Mind That Burns in Each Body': Women, Rape, and Racial Violence," *Southern Exposure* 12 (1984): 64.

[10] Joel Williamson, *The Crucible of Race: Black-White Relations in the American South since Emancipation* (New York: Oxford University Press, 1984), 117.

[11] Frederick Douglass, "Lessons of the Hour," 1894, 22–23, Stone/60:26, Alfred Stone Collection, Mississippi Department of Archives and History, Jackson, Mississippi, 24.

to create and reinforce racial difference. Beginning in the mid- to late 1880s, Southern state legislatures began passing Jim Crow laws that excluded or segregated blacks in railroad cars, restaurants, hotels, movie theaters, recreation facilities, schools, hospitals, and cemeteries. Jim Crow laws separated blacks and whites in public spaces in order to enforce a hierarchical and systematic racial-class system of oppression that was designed to perpetuate white supremacy and black social, economic, and political degradation. Just as segregating blacks in public spaces intended to impose clear racial boundaries between blacks and whites, the racialization of lynching was about reserving lynching for "inferior" black bodies and making "superior" white bodies safe from lynching.

The racialization of lynching had a profound impact on the kinds of lynching narratives black Americans crafted. Prior to the racialization of lynching, black vigilantes lynched other blacks for alleged violent crimes and especially violent crimes carried out against black women and children. Available evidence suggests that black vigilantes believed the lynching of alleged black criminals was necessary or warranted. However, because of the emergence of the black beast rapist discourse and the stigma it attached to black lynch victims, black commentators began to portray black vigilantism as dangerous and ill-advised and ridiculed blacks who participated in it. The black commentators suggested that black vigilantism implied black support for white-on-black lynching and the racist discourses that rationalized it. In addition, the racialization of lynching compelled black Americans to craft counternarratives to racist depictions of black lynch victims found in mainstream American discourse. *Beyond the Rope* posits that black antilynching activists, writers, and ordinary people rejected the black beast rapist narrative and sought to displace it by constructing two distinct genres of lynching narratives: victimization narratives of the lynched black body and consoling narratives of the lynched black body. In the main, the victimization narratives of the lynched black body framed black lynch victims as dehumanized sufferers who were deserving of legal protection and sympathy, whereas the consoling narratives typically framed black lynch victims as heroic and thereby sought to inspire black Americans to fight back against their oppression or to remember black lynch victims in empowering ways. In examining how black Americans have negotiated and renegotiated the meaning of the lynched black body across the long twentieth century, I intend to show how black perspectives concerning the lynched black body have evolved in response to particular historical and rhetorical circumstances. *Beyond the Rope* begins in the early 1880s, when African Americans had not yet become the primary targets of lynch mob violence and lynching was not yet the dominant symbol of white supremacy. Using primarily newspaper reports of black vigilantism in the Mississippi and Arkansas Deltas (the statistical epicenter of black vigilantism), Chapter 1 charts the legal, political, and social dynamics that shaped the rise and decline of black vigilantism. It explains the spike in black vigilantism during the mid- to late 1880s. It also demonstrates that rape and murder were the predominant allegations that precipitated black vigilantism, which suggests that black Americans believed those particular crimes warranted lynching. However, the chapter shows how, by the 1890s, white-on-black lynch mob violence soared and racist representations of the lynched black body as beast were increasingly employed to justify lynching. I argue that these developments compelled black Americans to craft lynching narratives that condemned black vigilantism and also led to African Americans abstaining from lynching other blacks after the 1880s – because black extralegal violence might have implied black support for white-on-black lynching and the racist discourses with which it was rationalized.

Chapter 2 shifts the focus away from the black vigilantism of the 1880s and its subsequent decline and instead examines how black activists and black communities organized defense campaigns to save potential lynch victims and reframed black lynch victims as innocent, helpless victims (rather than black beast rapists) in response to the crisis of white-on-black lynch mob violence. Specifically, Chapter 2 primarily tells the story of a significant but largely forgotten antilynching defense campaign. Henry Lowery, a black sharecropper, was accused of brutally murdering a wealthy Arkansas planter on Christmas Day 1920. With the help of local blacks, Lowery escaped to El Paso, Texas, one thousand miles away, where he was arrested, released into Arkansas authorities' custody, captured by a posse en route to Arkansas, and subsequently burned at the stake. The chapter chronicles Lowery's and the NAACP's efforts to prevent a lynching in the making and analyzes Lowery's fateful decision to waive extradition proceedings in exchange for the promise of safe passage to Arkansas and a fair trial. Chapter 2 concludes with a discussion of the NAACP's efforts to utilize the Henry Lowery lynching as a focal point of its ongoing lobbying efforts for a federal antilynching law. It particularly notes how the NAACP's "An American Lynching" pamphlet sought to counter representations of Lowery as a "desperado negro" and instead reframed him as a helpless and dehumanized victim of lynch mob violence in order to provoke white outrage and authenticate black suffering.

Although useful for certain antilynching aims, the lynched black body as a victimized subject had little value for blacks attempting to cope with the trauma of lynching. Chapter 3 explores how literary representations framed the lynched black body as a symbol of manly defiance. Through an analysis of seminal works such as Sutton Griggs's novel *The Hindered Hand: Or the Rein of the Repressionist* and Richard Wright's novellas in *Uncle Tom's Children*, this chapter demonstrates how black writers constructed consoling narratives of the lynched black body that simultaneously advanced counternarratives to heroic portrayals of white mob violence and narratives of the lynched black body as a dehumanized victim by imagining black lynch victims as symbolizing black manhood through armed resistance to white lynch mob violence. In addition, my analysis of literary consoling narratives of the lynched black body reveals the complex cultural politics of resisting lynching by highlighting black Americans' attitudes concerning armed self-defense, moral suasion, and legalism as appropriate responses to racial violence.

Whereas Chapter 3 privileges literary narratives, Chapter 4 examines how black Americans constructed consoling narratives of the lynched black body in oral memory. Black oral histories highlight the brutalization of family members and friends by white lynch mob violence, but they also emphasize black agency when they describe escaping mob violence or violently confronting a lynch mob. Most notably, blacks reminisced that if they had been lynched, they would have killed as many whites as possible in the process. In these ways, black memories transformed lynchings into occasions that bore witness to black agency rather than victimhood. Although *Beyond the Rope* dedicates more consideration to the armed resistance to white lynch mob violence in its discussion of consoling narratives of the lynched black body, it should be noted that armed resistance is only one index of human agency; black Americans have pursued various approaches to confronting lynching – such as mobilizing indignation meetings and lobbying Congress for passage of an antilynching law.[12]

In sum, *Beyond the Rope* utilizes the lens of black-authored narratives of the lynched black body to unearth the multiple, and often conflicting, relationships that black Americans have had with lynching and the lynched black body. Black Americans' relationship to the lynched black body has ranged from black Americans lynching other black Americans to being victims of white-on-black lynch mob violence. Due to black Americans' varied and complex relationships to the lynched black body, they have had to develop different representational strategies for dealing with it. Emphasizing how black Americans employed or represented the lynched black body at different times for different rhetorical effects is important, because it highlights that the lynched black body in the black cultural imagination should be seen as a floating signifier rather than a static, one-dimensional symbol of black death or white terror. Although black Americans have framed lynched black bodies as symbols of black death and white terror – and continue to do so – they have also framed lynched black bodies as affirmations of black subjectivity and humanity. In this way, *Beyond the Rope* attempts to explain the shifting historical and rhetorical contexts that gave rise to differing narratives of the lynched black body over the long twentieth century.

12 Jocelyn A. Hollander and Rachel L. Einwohner, "Conceptualizing Resistance," *Sociological Forum* 19 (2004): 545.

1

Black Vigilantism

Prior to the racialization of lynching in the mid- to late 1880s, black Americans understood black vigilantism in light of warranted lynchings carried out in response to certain violent crimes. By "warranted lynchings," I am referring to the ways in which black vigilantism was understood as a necessary and legitimate response to alleged violent crimes that were precipitated by black persons. However, after lynching became a racialized phenomenon, black-authored narratives about black vigilantism increasingly suggested that instances of black vigilantism were unwarranted, regardless of the precipitating allegation. The reason was that black vigilantism lent tacit support to the black beast rapist narrative and undermined black-authored victimization narratives of the lynched black body. Here I argue that black-authored narratives about black vigilantism that condemned it occurred in response to the racialization of lynching.

This chapter is organized around explaining the social and political logic that informed black vigilantism and how that logic unraveled in the face of the racialization of lynching. The first section begins by providing a brief overview of the broad social and political motivations that gave rise to black vigilantism in the South, carefully examining the history of black vigilantism in the Mississippi and Arkansas Delta regions. The experience in the Deltas is a useful lens for exploring the dynamics that resulted in black vigilantism, because approximately one-third of all documented instances of black vigilantism occurred in those areas. In addition, the first section analyzes particular instances of black vigilantism in the Mississippi and Arkansas Deltas and the allegations that provoked them. In charting the allegations that gave rise to black vigilantism, the goal is to explain the circumstances in which black vigilantes believed lynching another black person was warranted. The chapter's second section explains how and why the racialization of lynching precipitated the decline of black vigilantism and especially how it impacted black-authored narratives about black vigilantism.

BLACK VIGILANTISM AS WARRANTED LYNCHINGS

The Social and Political Context for Black Vigilantism

According to sociologists Stewart Tolnay and E. M. Beck's inventory of Southern lynching, between 1882 and 1930, black vigilantes executed approximately 148 persons across ten Southern states.[1] Of those 148 victims of black vigilantism, 54 were executed in the Mississippi and Arkansas Deltas (see map in Figure 3).[2] The inventory of black vigilantism in the Delta region includes at least 14 lynch victims who were executed by interracial vigilante groups (composed of blacks and whites). My analysis of interracial mobs suggests that they should be treated separately from exclusively black vigilante groups because it is difficult to gauge the degree of black participation and whether it was voluntary or coerced. Therefore, when interracial lynch mobs are excluded, I estimate that black vigilantes executed approximately 36 individuals in the Mississippi and Arkansas Deltas.

The criminal justice system's failure to prosecute crimes perpetrated against blacks is the primary context for understanding why black vigilantism occurred. This dynamic encouraged extralegal

[1] Stewart E. Tolnay and E. M. Beck, *A Festival of Violence: An Analysis of Southern Lynchings, 1882–1930* (Urbana: University of Illinois Press, 1995), 93.

[2] The approximate number of victims of black vigilantism in ten Southern states: Mississippi (49), Louisiana (23), Arkansas (21), Georgia (13), Alabama (11), Florida (11), Kentucky (10), North Carolina (7), South Carolina (6), Tennessee (2). A comprehensive inventory of Southern lynch victims between the years 1882 and 1930 can be accessed online at Project HAL (Historical American Lynching Data Collection Project), http://people.uncw.edu/hinese/HAL/HAL%20Web%20Page.htm. According to Project HAL, their lynching data is derived from NAACP records at the Tuskegee Institute in Tuskegee, Alabama. Stewart Tolnay and E. M. Beck examined these records for name and event duplication and other errors, with funding from a National Science Foundation grant, and made their findings available to Project HAL in 1998.

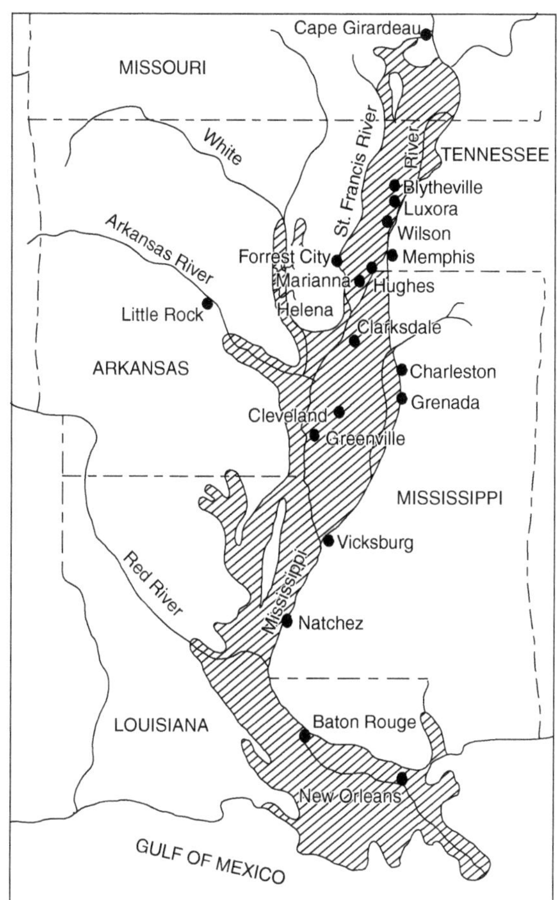

FIGURE 3 Map of the Lower Mississippi River Valley
Source: Redrawn/created by publisher.

violence in the Deltas as well as in other regions of the South. During congressional Reconstruction (1868–1877), blacks participated in the legal system in unprecedented numbers. In Warren County, Mississippi, blacks accounted for at least 50 percent of grand jurors between 1870 and 1873.[3] Despite this exceptional participation of

[3] Christopher Waldrep, *Roots of Disorder: Race and Criminal Justice in the American South, 1817–80* (Urbana: University of Illinois Press, 1998), 133. According to Waldrep, during presidential Reconstruction, blacks were excluded from grand jury service. Although black grand juror participation dramatically

blacks on grand juries during Reconstruction, however, over 70 percent of prosecutions in this period involved white victims and white defendants, whereas no more than 8 percent of all cases involved black victims and black/white defendants.[4] Among all cases of murder in which the race of the victim can be identified, 66 percent involved white victims and defendants.[5] In addition, grand juries indicted people for the murder of whites 50 percent more often than for the murder of blacks. Given that blacks in Warren County tended to commit crimes against persons and whites more frequently committed crimes against property, these statistics suggest that even under the best circumstances, crimes perpetrated against blacks were seldom prosecuted.[6]

Moreover, as congressional Reconstruction was overturned in the Delta region during the late 1870s and replaced by conservative, white Democratic regimes in the 1880s, black grand jury representation (along with black office holding) declined precipitously. For example, from 1873 onward, whites in Warren County, Mississippi (particularly Vicksburg, Mississippi), consciously chose lawlessness and extralegal violence, for the purpose of ousting blacks from local offices. Thus, by 1874, black grand jury representation shrank to 25 percent of total participation. White jurors increasingly resisted returning many indictments based upon black complaints.[7] According to historian Edward Ayers, "the injustice of Southern courts ... whites increasingly admitted, alienated blacks, [and] made them see the law as white law."[8] Anecdotal evidence from the Mississippi Delta supports this observation. According to historian John C. Willis, a white merchant named Pat Dean established himself as a one-man legal system by appointing himself justice of the peace in Merigold, Mississippi (Bolivar County). In that capacity, Dean did not consider murder a serious offense, particularly if the victim was black. During the early 1890s when a white railroad agent

increased during congressional Reconstruction, blacks were still underrepresented, given that in 1870, blacks constituted 70 percent of Warren County's total population.

4 Ibid., 136.

5 Ibid., 144.

6 Ibid., 132.

7 Ibid., 146 and 167.

8 Edward Ayers, *Vengeance and Justice: Crime and Punishment in the 19th Century American South* (New York: Oxford University Press, 1984), 230.

murdered a black man in Merigold, Dean fined the railroad agent five dollars and bragged that he would not attempt to collect the fine. According to Willis, in response to Pat Dean's slight, "every man carried his own weapons and was his own peacemaker."[9] Under these circumstances, Mississippi and Arkansas Delta blacks likely felt compelled to take the law into their own hands due to the arbitrary nature of the criminal justice system.

The Identity of Black Vigilantes and Their Victims

In a span of two weeks, two black persons went missing in Keo, Arkansas, in 1910. These individuals were Frank Pride's and Laura Mitchell's spouses. According to a newspaper report, the Pride and Mitchell families lived and worked on neighboring plantations. Shortly after both disappearances, a justice of the peace questioned Frank Pride about his wife's whereabouts. In response, Pride stated that his wife was visiting relatives in nearby Conway, Arkansas. Friends of Pride's wife later learned that the relatives the wife was supposedly visiting had been dead for many years. Reportedly, very shortly after their spouses' disappearance, Laura Mitchell and Frank Pride left their respective plantations in Keo, found work on a nearby plantation, and had been living together ever since. Despite their departure from the scene, the search for their spouses continued. Blacks in Keo suspected foul play and searched for Laura Mitchell's husband (Wiley Mitchell) on the plantation where Frank Pride had recently been employed. During their search, they discovered Wiley Mitchell's body buried in a garden plot that had belonged to Frank Pride. Wiley Mitchell appeared to have been bludgeoned to death with a club, which was later found in a nearby forest. Upon locating Mitchell's body, suspicion was immediately focused on Frank Pride.[10]

Subsequently, both Laura Mitchell and Frank Pride were arrested and a preliminary hearing was held. At the hearing, Mitchell and Pride apparently told "conflicting stories" about the death of Wiley Mitchell and the disappearance of Frank Pride's wife. The newspaper report does not detail their statements, but their inconsistent accounts apparently caused blacks in attendance to

[9] John Willis, *Forgotten Time: The Yazoo-Mississippi Delta after the Civil War* (Charlottesville: University of Virginia Press, 2000), 43.

[10] "Negroes Lynched by a Mob of Negroes," *Little Rock Arkansas Gazette*, April 6, 1910.

emphatically threaten to lynch the pair, for which purpose they immediately organized outside the courthouse. Given that Mitchell and Pride quickly moved away from Keo and moved in together, it is likely that blacks interpreted Mitchell's and Pride's "conflicting stories" as an attempt to conceal a conspiracy to kill their spouses so that they could be together.[11]

Based upon their preliminary trial testimony, the local magistrate charged both Pride and Mitchell with first-degree murder pending a formal grand jury investigation and trial. Because blacks had threatened to lynch Pride and Mitchell, a constable (presumably with armed police officers) was tasked with secreting them out of town. However, en route to their designated safe haven outside of Keo, a group of black vigilantes cornered them and forced the constable to hand over the pair. It was reported that within minutes, the vigilantes broke the shackles, hung the prisoners from a nearby tree, and riddled their bodies with bullets.[12]

The 1910 Frank Pride and Laura Mitchell lynching typified certain features of black vigilantism throughout the Delta region but differed in other respects. Similar to this lynching, the majority of alleged crimes that precipitated black vigilantism occurred on plantations or involved persons connected with the plantation economy. However, whereas the Mitchell and Pride lynching involved a married female farm laborer, victims of black vigilantism tended in general to be black males – young, married, and employed as farm laborers. The average age of lynch victims was thirty-three years, 88 percent were designated as farmers or farm laborers (the occupation of eight of nine lynch victims was listed), and 93 percent were married (the marital status of thirteen of fourteen lynch victims was listed).[13]

[11] Ibid.

[12] Ibid.

[13] I identified the following seven lynch victims from the Mississippi Delta: James Green, Mose Lemons, Dennis Martin, Raymond Murphy, Allen Nance, Sandy Wallace, and Columbus White. From the Arkansas Delta, I identified the following eight lynch victims: Eugene Baker, John Barnett, Robert Donnelly, John Farmer, Edward Hardy, Henry Jones, Laura Mitchell, and David Scruggs. For complete census information on these individuals, see: Ancestry.com, s.v. "Sandy Wallace," 1870 United States Federal Census [database online] (Provo: The Generations Network, 2003); ibid., s.vv. "James Green," "Laura Mitchell," and "Allen Nance," 1900 United States Federal Census [database online] (Provo: The Generations Network, 2004); and ibid., s.v. "Edward Hardy," 1910 United States Federal Census [database online] (Provo: The Generations Network, 2006).

Given that the alleged crimes tended to occur on plantations, it is likely that black vigilantes and their victims knew each other. In connection with this point, it is important to note that black vigilante activity peaked at a time when black settlements were undergoing a transformation from a concentrated pattern associated with the Old South plantation economy to a more dispersed or scattered distribution. Charles Aiken, geographer and historian, argues that in the aftermath of the Civil War, large cotton plantations (particularly in the Delta region) were subdivided into smaller allotments, which, depending on the size of the plantation, could be divided among several black families.[14] In general, black sharecroppers and agricultural wageworkers lived on plantations. If a critical mass of black families settled on a particular plantation (or set of plantations), they established community institutions such as churches or meeting places on the grounds of the plantation. Social bonds and ties were most often nurtured by these community institutions and networks. Yet although black institutions were primarily sites for community building and a refuge from white domination, they could also facilitate the formation of black vigilante groups.

For example, in 1923, Ed Hardy allegedly murdered an aged black woman on a plantation in Tunica County, Mississippi. The plantation supervisor and his assistant captured Hardy, who had fled to Arkansas. They returned Hardy to the plantation and notified the local police of his capture. While the plantation workers were waiting for police to arrive and arrest the suspect, a group of black vigilantes reportedly kidnapped Hardy, bludgeoned him, and threw his body into the Mississippi River. According to a newspaper report, the murdered woman was well liked by both whites and blacks, and black plantation workers were "greatly excited" by her murder.[15] Even though the composition of the group of black vigilantes and their relationship to the murdered

For the remaining lynch victims, see, ibid., 1880 Federal Census [database online] (Provo: The Generations Network, 2005). I identified two additional lynch victims in marriage records: see Ancestry.com, s.v. "Frank King," Arkansas Marriages, 1779–1992 [database online] (Provo: The Generations Network, 2004), and, ibid., s.v. "Thomas Mack," Mississippi Marriages, 1776–1935 [database online] (Provo: Generations Network, 2004).

14 Charles Aiken, *The Cotton Plantation South since the Civil War* (Baltimore: Johns Hopkins University Press, 1998), 39–49.

15 "Negroes Lynch Negro, Slayer of Old Mammy," *Memphis Commercial Appeal*, November 11, 1923.

black woman is unclear, it seems likely that the vigilantes were mostly comprised of blacks who worked on the same plantation as the victim. In fact, newspaper reports typically depicted black vigilante groups as small contingents, mainly made up of family and friends of alleged victims. For example, only two black vigilante incidents were reported in which the number of participants exceeded twenty people.[16] It seems likely, then, that the murdered black woman's family and fellow plantation workers were "greatly excited" because they were angered by her death and revenged it by lynching Ed Hardy.

Black vigilantes in the Delta region were almost exclusively activated by violent crimes. Murder constituted 61 percent (or twenty-two of thirty-six incidents) of allegations that precipitated black vigilante lynchings in the Delta region, whereas murder triggered approximately 45 percent of black vigilantism in the South as a whole. In the Mississippi and Arkansas Deltas, murders that led to lynchings oftentimes followed on the heels of domestic conflicts. In two cases, black vigilantes lynched a black man who had murdered a companion or a companion's relative. In 1907, Andrew Trice allegedly brutally murdered his mistress in Desoto County, Mississippi. It was reported that Trice dispatched the woman with an axe and tossed her body into the Mississippi River. In response to this murder, a group of vigilantes comprising thirty blacks removed Trice from police custody and subsequently lynched him and tossed his body into the river at the place where it was believed that he had concealed his victim's body.[17] In another example, in 1887, Lloyd Martin allegedly assaulted his wife and murdered Bob Jones, his wife's father, in Sunflower County, Mississippi. Following this incident, a mob of black vigilantes seized Martin from the police and lynched him.[18]

It is interesting to note that in at least one case, black vigilantes lynched a white person for the murder of a black man. For instance, in May 1884, Samuel T. Wilson, a white convict guard, allegedly murdered Negia McDaniel, a black fisherman, in Issaquena County, Mississippi. According to a newspaper report, Wilson and a crew of black convict laborers under his command were hauling lumber

[16] For those two incidents, see "Two Negro Incendiaries Lynched, "*Times Picayune*, March 3, 1887, and *The Daily Picayune*, February 24, 1913.

[17] *Atlanta Constitution*, July 21, 1907.

[18] *Atlanta Constitution*, July 27, 1887.

aboard a river flatboat.[19] Wilson and his crew landed near McDaniel, who happened to be fishing. It was reported that Wilson and McDaniel exchanged hostile words, and in response, Wilson ordered two black convict laborers to take McDaniel aboard the flatboat, beat him, and throw him overboard. In response to the alleged crime, Wilson was arrested and arraigned before Adam Jenkins, a black justice of the peace, who reportedly only allowed testimony from two black witnesses and refused to allow persons "friendly" with Wilson to testify. Based upon the testimony of the two black witnesses, Jenkins ruled that a grand jury should decide Wilson's fate. Upon hearing the two black eyewitnesses implicate Wilson in McDaniel's murder, three hundred blacks (in attendance at the hearing) shouted so emphatically that they intended to lynch Wilson that Jenkins requested Deputy Sheriff Lawson, a white officer, to escort Wilson out of town, presumably to a nearby jail. By the time Lawson arrived, tensions appeared to have calmed; however, once Wilson was in custody, a group of black vigilantes forced Lawson and his armed guard to hand over Wilson, approximately a half mile from the hearing's location. Wasting very little time, the black vigilantes lynched Wilson and left his body hanging for days afterward.[20]

In the days following the Wilson lynching, white newspapers in the Mississippi Delta roundly condemned it, albeit for different reasons. According to the *Grenada Sentinel*, "Mob rule has gotten to be so common all over the country that negroes are taking to it to avenge real and fancied injuries." The paper went on to say, "Mob law is as good and righteous in the hands of negroes as it is in white people, but is violently, flagrantly, hellishly wrong in either."[21] An editorial from the *Greenville Times* registered a qualified condemnation of the Wilson lynching, which hinged upon race. "The citizens of Issaquena county may well be exercised over this, the third lynching in their small county in one year. As to this atrocious wretch, Wilson, he deserved death and torture."[22] However, the editorial lamented,

[19] For a detailed analysis of the convict lease system in Mississippi, see Edward Ayers, *Vengeance and Justice*, and Vernon Lane Wharton, *The Negro in Mississippi, 1865–1890* (New York: Harper and Row, 1965).

[20] "Vicksburg," *Times Picayune*, April 29, 1884; "Judge Lynch," *Chicago Daily Tribune*, April 29, 1884. For another example of black vigilantes lynching a white man, see Bruce Baker, "Lynch Law Reversed," 273–293.

[21] "Mob Law," *Vicksburg Evening Post*, May 19, 1884.

[22] "The Issaquena County Lynching," *Greenville Times*, May 10, 1884.

These affairs are the natural outgrowth of the feeble administration of justice which has unfortunately prevailed in this judicial district for years past. And indulged in Issaquena without restriction or even a pretense at correction or punishment, they are sure to be more commonly resorted to; and regarded as the proper and permissible recourse for the correction of crime. The last lynching [Samuel Wilson's] is attended by added cause of alarm. If ever lynching is excusable by the enormity of any crime, it is when it is resorted to by the best representatives of a community's intelligence and conscience. . . . Those are not found among the negro masses. Nor yet is this the most serious feature of the hanging of the white brute. The white supremacy and dominance of the white race is maintained in the black belt in a great measure by fear. This dominance is to be maintained at any and all costs. It is imperiled by permitting the killing of any white man by a negro or negroes for any cause except self-defense or defense of family; to go unpunished.[23]

Unlike the *Grenada Sentinel* editorial, the *Greenville Times* column supported the lynching of Samuel Wilson in principle but deplored it in practice because it might imply that black people could kill whites with impunity, which would ostensibly pose problems for the white minority in maintaining dominance over the black majority in the Mississippi Delta. The editorial ended by demanding that the Washington County grand jury impaneled to investigate the Samuel Wilson lynching punish all blacks who participated in the lynching. However, after the appearance of this editorial, no extant newspaper coverage of the case can be found; therefore, the ultimate fate of the black vigilantes who lynched Wilson is unclear.

It also appears that black vigilantes were provoked by blacks who murdered or attempted to murder for the purpose of ridding themselves of a competing lover. In 1889, a group of nine black men beat and killed Dan Reynolds near Coffee Creek, Arkansas. According to a newspaper report, the black vigilantes murdered Reynolds because he had a relationship with a popular woman. The lynchers beat Reynolds with barbed wire, rubbed mud on his wounds, and left him for dead. Reynolds barely survived the initial attack, but subsequently died from the wounds he suffered. Prior to his death, he named three of his attackers, which eventually led to the arrest of seven of the nine. According to reports, the black community was incensed by the brutal murder, and "there [was] strong talk among them of lynching the miscreants. . . ."[24] Also, in

[23] Ibid.
[24] "Negro White Caps," *Little Rock Arkansas Gazette*, January 15, 1889.

1895, Frank King, a black pastor, allegedly shot and killed William Toney, a deacon, in Portland, Arkansas. Apparently, trouble between King and Toney was precipitated by King's infatuation with Toney's wife. Whether Toney violently confronted King is unclear; however, a confrontation occurred and resulted in King shooting Toney in the abdomen. Purportedly, "King was locked up and after dark a mob of infuriated negroes repaired to the lockup, took King to a tree and lynched him."[25]

In addition, black vigilantes executed black men who murdered other black people as a result of work-related disputes. Although specific details related to the disputes that led to the murders are unknown, two murders that led to lynching occurred at work sites. In 1905, John Barnett allegedly quarreled with and killed Albert Wakefield (both of whom were levee workers) in Lee County, Arkansas. In response, a group of twenty black men captured Barnett and hung him from a tree.[26] In another example, Henry Gentry allegedly murdered George Hillyard on the Palmyra plantation in Warren County, Mississippi in 1891. It was reported that Gentry was arrested and being escorted to trial by two armed guards when black vigilantes overpowered the guards, seized Gentry, and hung him.[27]

Besides murder, rape accounted for 31 percent (or eleven of thirty-six) of black vigilante incidents.[28] My analysis revealed that approximately 82 percent of rape allegations involved black children. In 1892, Robert Donnelly allegedly raped a twelve-year-old girl in Lee County, Arkansas. In the 1880 census, Robert Donnelly was listed as a married farmworker with four sons and one daughter.[29] With the exception of his youngest son, he and his family members were born in Georgia. Evidently, the unidentified girl survived Donnelly's attack and informed her parents about what had occurred. The girl's parents reported the crime, Donnelly was arrested, and a preliminary hearing was conducted in which

[25] *Fort Wayne News*, June 21, 1895.

[26] "Negroes Lynch a Negro," *Little Rock Arkansas Gazette*, April 21, 1905.

[27] "A Negro Lynched," *Daily Picayune*, July 8, 1891.

[28] In addition to murder and rape allegations, three blacks were lynched for other reasons. Frank King was lynched for shooting a man and adultery; Ernest Williams was lynched for obscene language and Columbus White was lynched for arson. For complete information on these lynchings, see Project HAL, http://people.uncw.edu/hinese/HAL/HAL%20Web%20Page.htm.

[29] Ancestry.com, s.v. "Robert Donnelly," 1880 Federal Census [database online] (Provo: The Generations Network, 2005).

Donnelly was found guilty of the crime. In response, a group of black vigilantes assembled, forced open his cell, and hung him from a nearby tree.[30]

When incidents of alleged rape and murder committed against black women and children are combined, they represent approximately 50 percent of the total allegations that led to lynching. These statistics suggest that black vigilantes may have been activated by a masculine ethos to protect women and children, who were deemed dependents of male protection. In the post–Civil War South (particularly in the Mississippi Delta), blacks understood the household as the foundation for their freedom. As the legal heads of household, black men had patriarchal power over their wives and children, which allowed them to claim ownership of their dependents' labor. Moreover, black men's wives and children became the symbol of their manhood and the basis upon which they could claim social and political equality with white men.[31] Given this context, it is possible that black men interpreted sexual and violent crimes against women as attacks on their manhood. Therefore, through lynching, black vigilantes enforced black masculine control over the household, to which protection of women and children was central.

Black vigilantes typically eschewed rituals of violence associated with spectacle lynching such as mutilation, castration, and burning. This is likely so because the main objective of the vigilantes was to rid themselves of dangerous criminals. Although black vigilantes typically hung or shot alleged criminals, in one instance they mutilated an alleged rapist. At the time of the lynching, David Scruggs was a forty-two-year-old married farmer with two daughters (aged ten and eleven).[32] Scruggs was arrested in Jefferson County, Arkansas, in 1885 for accusations of incest with one of his daughters. When Scruggs failed to provide bail, he was returned to jail. However, he apparently "sued out a writ of *habeas corpus*" to a circuit judge and was released. In response to his release, black vigilantes captured and lynched Scruggs. According to a news report, the "negroes ... carved him to pieces with knives,

[30] "His Black Neck," *Little Rock Arkansas Gazette*, July 1, 1892.

[31] Nancy Bercaw, *Gendered Freedoms: Race, Rights, and the Politics of Household in the Delta, 1861–1875* (Gainesville: University Press of Florida, 2003), 99–116.

[32] Ancestry.com, s.v. "David Scruggs," 1880 Federal Census [database online] (Provo: The Generations Network, 2005).

and the most unusual wounds inflicted on him," and he subsequently "crept away in the woods and died."[33]

In another example, black vigilantes reportedly set on fire a lynch victim. In 1893, Dan T. Nelson was accused of murdering Ben Betts in Lincoln County, Arkansas. It was reported that Betts went to Nelson's home to collect a rent payment. Betts and Nelson quarreled over the rent payment to such a degree that Nelson shot and killed Betts. Purportedly, in response to the Betts murder, "the negroes [were] worked up to a fever pitch-heat over the affair." Furthermore, the newspaper report stated, "the mob secured a long piece of steel ... and with this battered down the door of the jail. This accomplished, they had no difficulty securing the prisoner. The men were armed with Winchesters, and as soon as Nelson was taken out of the jail, they leveled their guns and filled his body with lead. They then threw him on a pile of trash and set his clothes on fire."[34] It is unclear why David Scruggs was mutilated or Dan Nelson's body was set on fire, given that other lynch victims who committed similar crimes were not. Despite a few instances of black vigilantes mutilating their victims or setting them ablaze, the primary function of black vigilantism was punitive rather than terroristic – whereas white-on-black lynch mob violence was both punitive and terroristic.[35]

Although it is uncertain why some black vigilantes mutilated or set their victims on fire, by and large, it seems evident that black vigilantes lynched other blacks because they believed violent crimes warranted lynching. Perhaps the most compelling evidence of this belief is the fact that black vigilante groups typically lynched their victims after they had already been arrested. On average, Southern black vigilantes removed alleged criminals from police custody approximately 40 percent of the time; however, black vigilante groups in the Mississippi Delta removed 64 percent (or twenty-three of thirty-six) of lynch victims from police custody.

[33] "Unnatural Father Lynched by His Colored Brethren," *Little Rock Daily Gazette*, July 25, 1885. See the following newspaper articles for the remaining four rape allegations that involved children: "Strung Him Up," *Little Rock Arkansas Gazette*, July 15, 1892; "A Negro Ravisher Lynched," *Times Picayune*, July 1, 1885; *Times Democrat*, November 18, 1890; *Commercial Appeal*, September 20, 1903.

[34] "Bullets and Fire," *Little Rock Arkansas Gazette*, November 15, 1893.

[35] For an elaboration on this point, see Terence Finnegan, *A Deed So Accursed: Lynchings in Mississippi and South Carolina, 1881–1940* (Charlottesville: University of Virginia Press, 2013), 151.

In Mississippi as a whole, approximately 60 percent of black vigilante incidents involved removing alleged criminals from police custody.[36] Although it might appear on the surface that black vigilantes who removed alleged criminals from police custody were motivated by the same reasons as white vigilantes, upon closer inspection, it is clear that white vigilantism and black vigilantism emanate from different sources. In the main, white vigilantes claimed that they sidestepped the legal system because it did not punish alleged criminals quickly or severely enough, even though, according to historian Margaret Vandiver, "the overwhelming majority of lynchings occurred in precisely the one category of case where the criminal justice system dependably acted with great speed, certainty, and severity – cases in which African Americans were accused of crimes against whites."[37] Even when the criminal justice system hastily arrested, tried, and convicted blacks for crimes against whites, white vigilantes often forcibly removed blacks from state custody and lynched them because they believed that lynch mobs were the supreme and truest expression of the will of the people.[38] In contrast, evidence suggests that black vigilantes circumvented the criminal justice system because it rarely punished crimes perpetrated against blacks. Therefore, whites lynched because they fundamentally disagreed with *how* the legal system adjudicated crimes, whereas black vigilantes lynched because they believed the criminal justice system *ignored* criminal activity committed against blacks. The fact that black vigilantes lynched alleged criminals after they had been taken into police custody speaks to how deeply black Americans distrusted the criminal justice system. For example, in response to news in August 1894 that black vigilantes had lynched a white man, Ida B. Wells (who later became a well-known activist) reflected that "a white man lynched by negroes is such an unusual thing that one can scarcely believe it is true." Yet Wells seemingly rationalized the acts of black vigilantes when she observed that "the negroes in West Virginia may have been morally certain that the white man would never be

[36] Ibid.

[37] Margaret Vandiver, *Lethal Punishment: Lynchings and Legal Executions in the South* (New Brunswick: Rutgers University Press, 2006), 90.

[38] For a more elaborate explanation of the motivational and philosophical dynamics that produced white vigilantism, see Waldrep, *African Americans Confront Lynching*; Vandiver, *Lethal Punishment*; Pfeifer, *Rough Justice*; and Rushdy, *American Lynching*.

punished for his crime by judge or jury, who are always white."[39] Therefore, if Edward Ayers's observation is correct that whites' apathy toward crimes perpetrated against blacks created a perception among blacks that the formal legal system represented "white law," it should come as no surprise that blacks eschewed "white law" even when it seemed to be adjudicating crimes perpetrated against blacks.

In sum, black vigilante violence in the Delta region was primarily carried out against young black male farm laborers who allegedly committed violent crimes. Given that violent crimes committed against blacks were seldom punished, it makes sense that these crimes represent the bulk of allegations that typically produced black vigilantism. Although the criminal justice system's failure to prosecute violent crimes committed against blacks likely encouraged vigilantism, it also seems that black vigilantes believed that murder and rape – particularly when women and children were the victims – warranted lynching. Moreover, after emancipation, Delta black males were legal heads of household and likely interpreted violent attacks on black women and children as attacks on their manhood. Given this background, it appears that black vigilantism was primarily motivated by the desire to expunge dangerous criminals from the community, but in important ways it was also about (re)inscribing, through vigilante violence, patriarchal control over the household (which had been undermined by attacks on black women and children).

THE RACIALIZATION OF LYNCHING AND THE DECLINE OF BLACK VIGILANTISM

Beginning in the mid- to late 1880s, the number of white-on-black lynchings increased dramatically, and the number of white victims of vigilantism declined precipitously. The widening disparity between the numbers of white and black lynch victims after the mid-1880s reflected the racialization of lynch mob violence, in which black Americans became the primary targets of white lynch mob violence and antiblack rationales were employed to justify lynching. To be sure, this does not mean that instances of white-on-black lynching prior to the mid-1880s were not racially motivated. Rather, it means that in the

[39] J. Mitchell, *The Strangest Fruit: Forgotten Black-on-Black Lynchings, 1835–1935* (San Bernardino: CreateSpace Independent Publishing, 2010), 134.

wake of Reconstruction's defeat, whites increasingly employed lynching as a means to reassert white supremacy. Southern whites argued that lynching was necessary because black savages were raping white women in alarming numbers. More importantly, whites' widespread acceptance of the black beast rapist discourse transformed white-on-black lynching into a moral duty to protect white womanhood.[40] For example, between the years 1882 and 1889, 316 Southern blacks died at the hands of white lynch mobs. The following decade, approximately 744 black people (approximately a 300 percent increase) were executed by white mobs. During the period of 1882 to 1889, white-on-black lynch mob violence accounted for 72 percent of all lynching episodes, whereas white-on-white lynch mob violence accounted for 16 percent. A decade later, white-on-black lynch mob violence had increased to 82 percent of total lynching episodes, and white-on-white lynch mob violence had decreased to 12 percent (see Table 1). At the national level between the years 1882 and 1885, the number of whites lynched (411) far exceeded the number of blacks lynched (227). However, in the remainder of the nineteenth century, the number of blacks lynched increased from 227 to 1,524 (roughly a 600 percent increase), whereas white lynch victims increased from 411 to 696 (only a 69 percent increase) during the same period. Even those numbers do not entirely illustrate the extent to which blacks were becoming the primary targets of lynch mob violence, though, when one considers that in 1900, 106 blacks were lynched compared to only 9 whites.[41]

Consequently, the racialization of lynching impacted black-authored narratives about lynching in general and black vigilantism in particular. The ideological trajectory of Ida B. Wells, the foremost antilynching activist of the late nineteenth and early twentieth centuries, is a useful proxy for thinking about black Americans' relationship to lynching and the lynched black body prior to the racialization of lynching and afterward.[42] For

[40] For three excellent treatments of lynching and the "protection of womanhood" discourse, see Jacqueline Dowd Hall, *Revolt against Chivalry*; Crystal Feimster, *Southern Horrors: Women and the Politics of Rape and Lynching* (Cambridge: Harvard University Press, 2009); and Estelle B. Freedman, *Redefining Rape: Sexual Violence in the Era of Suffrage and Segregation* (Cambridge: Harvard University Press, 2013).

[41] For comprehensive lynching statistics between the years 1882 and 1968, see Zangrando, *The NAACP Crusade against Lynching*, 4–7.

[42] The secondary literature on Ida B. Wells is extensive. However, for detailed biographical treatments of Wells's life and activism, see Ida B. Wells-Barnett and

TABLE 1. *Number and Percentage of Lynch Victims by Decade, 1882–1930**

Year	Black Victim, Black Mob	Black Victim, White Mob	White Victim, White Mob	Percent Black Victim, Black Mob	Percent Black Victim, White Mob	Percent White Victim, White Mob
1882–1889	42	316	81	10	72	16
1890–1899	56	744	123	6	82	12
1900–1909	36	568	33	6	89	5
1910–1919	10	436	16	2	94	4
1920–1930	2	217	22	1	90	9

* Statistics are reflective of lynchings that occurred in Alabama, Arkansas, Florida, Georgia, Kentucky, Louisiana, Mississippi, North Carolina, South Carolina, and Tennessee.

Source: Adapted from Stewart E. Tolnay and E. M. Beck, *A Festival of Violence: An Analysis of Southern Lynchings, 1882–1930* (Urbana: University of Illinois Press, 1995, 271–272.

instance, in Wells's 1887 Memphis diary, she described a scandal that involved prominent white Memphians and suggested that the punishment fit the crime because the lady involved had been defamed by her male lover. Wells wrote,

> Another week has slipped away & I've done nothing. Interest has been & is still centered on the Godwin case that has brought forth some shocking developments concerning the morals of high life. A silly woman forgot her marriage vows for an equally scatterbrained boy; who boasted of his conquest in Nashville, St. Louis, Marianna, as well as here, as a result he lost his life. It seems awful to take human life but hardly more so than to take a woman's reputation & make it the jest & byword of the street; in view of these things, if he really did them, one is strongly tempted to say his killing was justifiable.[43]

Alfreda M. Duster, *Crusade for Justice: The Autobiography of Ida B. Wells* (Chicago: University of Chicago Press, 1991); Linda O. McCurry, *To Keep the Waters Troubled: The Life of Ida B. Wells* (New York: Oxford University Press, 2000); Patricia A. Schechter, *Ida B. Wells and American Reform, 1880–1930* (Chapel Hill: University of North Carolina Press, 2001); James West Davidson, *They Say: Ida B. Wells and the Reconstruction of Race* (New York: Oxford University Press, 2007); Paula J. Giddings, *Ida: A Sword among Lions: Ida B. Wells and the Campaign against Lynching* (New York: Harper, 2008); and Mia Bay, *To Tell the Truth Freely: The Life of Ida B. Wells* (New York: Hill and Wang, 2009).

43 Ida B. Wells-Barnett and Miriam Decosta-Willis, *The Memphis Diary of Ida B. Wells: An Intimate Portrait of the Activist as a Young Woman* (Boston: Beacon Press, 1995), 131–132.

As this quotation suggests, before the ascendancy of the black beast rapist discourse in the early 1890s, Wells believed that vigilantism was warranted in response to the defamation of womanhood, which would have included instances in which a woman had been assaulted or raped. Given that alleged rape and murder committed against black women and children accounted for approximately half of all allegations that precipitated black vigilantism, Wells's perspective on vigilantism vis-à-vis her 1887 diary entry is closely aligned to the rationales that motivated black vigilantism and indeed vigilantism more generally.

However, Wells's diary entry represents a black-authored narrative on vigilantism prior to black people, and particularly black men, having been stigmatized as black beast rapists. As the black beast rapist discourse took root by the early 1890s, and particularly when it became clear that it was merely a thinly veiled justification for segregation and disenfranchisement, Wells realized that lynching had become a tool of white supremacy. Specifically, Wells's antilynching activism sprang from witnessing the lynching of Thomas Moss, a successful black grocer, and two other black men in Memphis in 1892. What became clear for Wells was that the black beast rapist discourse did not simply rationalize the lynching of alleged black rapists; rather, it justified the wholesale attack on all black people, regardless of their social or economic attainment. Wells reflected,

> Like many another person who had read of lynching in the South, I had accepted the idea meant to be conveyed – that although lynching was irregular and contrary to law and order, unreasoning anger over the terrible crime of rape led to the lynching; that perhaps the brute deserved death anyhow and the mob was justified in taking his life.
>
> But Thomas Moss, Calvin McDowell, and Lee Stewart had been lynched in Memphis, one of the leading cities of the South, in which no lynching had taken place before, with just as much brutality as other victims of the mob; and they had committed no crime against women. This is what opened my eyes to what lynching really was. An excuse to get rid of Negroes who were acquiring wealth and property and thus keep the race terrorized and "keep the nigger down." I then began an investigation of every lynching I read about.[44]

Due to the changing social relations and cultural politics of lynching, Wells dramatically altered her thinking about vigilantism. Rather

[44] Wells and Duster, *Crusade for Justice*, 64.

than understanding the lynching of alleged black criminals, and particularly rapists, as warranted lynchings, Wells now believed that black lynch victims had been victimized by white lynch mobs. Rather than empathizing with lynchers, Wells became their chief opponent. Over the course of the next eight years, Wells penned three significant antilynching pamphlets that provocatively challenged the idea that black men were increasingly raping white women and that lynching was needed to deter black criminality and restore white womanhood.

Like Wells, other black Americans' attitudes toward lynching were transformed by the black beast rapist narrative and similarly awakened to "what lynching really was." In fact, Wells was not the only significant black leader to condemn the dramatic rise in white-on-black lynching at the turn of the century. In 1900, educator and philanthropist Booker T. Washington lamented how widespread lynching had become and in doing so acknowledged and condemned black vigilantism. Washington observed,

> The evil [lynching] has so grown that we are now at the point where not only blacks are lynched in the South, but white men as well. Not only this, but within the last six years at least a half-dozen coloured women have been lynched. And there are a few cases where Negroes have lynched members of their own race.[45]

When Booker T. Washington mentioned that the "evil has so grown," he is making a vague reference to the dramatic rise in white-on-black lynching, or what I refer to as the racialization of lynching. Washington attempted to underscore the growth by highlighting instances in which black women were lynched and "a few cases where Negroes have lynched members of their own race." In part, Washington attempted to make the case that all lynching is wrong regardless of the race of the lyncher or the race of the victim. Despite the fact that Washington stressed that there had been only a few cases of black vigilantism, he likely felt compelled to condemn those few instances because instances of black vigilantism (particularly for the allegation of rape) might have supported or reinforced white supremacist rationales for lynching. In this way, Washington firmly condemned rationales for white-on-black lynching and black vigilantism.

[45] J. Mitchell, *The Strangest Fruit*, 177.

Alongside Wells's and Washington's denunciations of white-on-black lynching and black vigilantism, the black press increasingly condemned black vigilantism after 1900. For example, a 1901 *Richmond Planet* editorial flatly asserted that "White mobs and colored mobs should be put on the same level, and be made to feel the strong corrective power of the law. Self-Preservation is the first law of nature, and should be exercised in dealing with unreasoning, bloodthirsty individuals, be they white or colored."[46] This particular black-authored narrative about black vigilantism stressed that lynchers, regardless of their race, should be held accountable. It is interesting to note that the *Richmond Planet* advanced this perspective even though by 1900 white-on-black lynch mob violence represented a far greater concern for black Americans. More strikingly, the *Richmond Planet* made this case even while knowing that the criminal justice system rarely treated white Americans and black Americans equally. However, with the advent of the racialization of lynching, and particularly the emergence of the black beast rapist narrative, the *Richmond Planet* – and by extension black Americans in general – came to believe that condemning black vigilantism was crucial to ultimately dismantling the cultural acceptance of lynching as a whole.

Even though black Americans increasingly condemned black vigilantism and white vigilantism with equal vigor, some black Americans feared that if black Americans were perceived to embrace black vigilantism, it might bolster apologists' rationales for white-on-black lynch mob violence as well as imperil black-authored victimization narratives of the lynched black body. With this in mind, a September 1903 *Colored American* editorial argued,

> We protest vigorously against lynchings, even of our confessed criminals, and against every other form of violence. Yet, we hear of a mob of Negroes lynching one of their own race down in Florida for assaulting a white woman, and of a most threatening demonstration by a crowd of colored excursionists down in Hot Springs, Ark., against the life of a colored speaker who was uttering some unpopular sentiments on the Jim Crow car question. The force of our compliant against the white man's inhumane and lawbreaking conduct is greatly weakened by occurrences like those referred to above.[47]

The *Colored American* editorial was concerned about both the perception of black Americans embracing vigilantism and of black

[46] Ibid., 204.
[47] Ibid., 218.

vigilantes seemingly lynching other blacks for alleged crimes that white mobs lynched black people for – for example, raping white women and challenging the status quo. For the *Colored American*, when black vigilantes lynched blacks for raping white women or challenging the status quo, black vigilantism tacitly sanctioned white-on-black lynching and reinforced racist rationales for lynching. To be sure, the editorial was not seeking to suggest that black vigilante activity that was precipitated by the rape of white women was somehow worse than black vigilantism that stemmed from the rape of black women. Rather, the point was that all black vigilantism was problematic; however, black vigilantism that was activated by alleged crimes that motivated white-on-black vigilantism severely weakened the idea that white-on-black vigilantism was somehow beyond the pale.

Even in the mid-1930s when the push for a federal antilynching bill was at its peak, black observers worried that relatively rare episodes of black vigilantism might potentially jeopardize congressional support for a federal antilynching bill. A 1934 *Chicago Defender* editorial entitled "Negro Lynchers" declared,

> Black America is seething with indignation this week because a mob of Negroes lynched another Negro [Grafton Page] at Shreveport, La. last Friday. The death of Grafton Page should not sabotage the fight against America's greatest evil. Instead, it should intensify it – especially among Negroes. In demanding the passage of an anti-lynching bill now, they will not only be fighting to protect themselves from others, they will be fighting to protect themselves from themselves.[48]

Black America seethed with anger because the belief was that black Americans could not hold whites accountable for lynching blacks if black Americans lynched blacks as well. More specifically, the *Chicago Defender* worried that if white America, and particularly congressional lawmakers, believed that white vigilantes were simply doing what black vigilantes did, how could black antilynching activists sustain their argument that white-on-black lynchings were racist and a systematic attempt to deprive black Americans of their civil rights? In addition, black vigilantism compromised the premise of lynching as a white racial oppression narrative because it suggested that lynching was not necessarily racially motivated or specifically motivated by white racism but rather a universal response to criminality. Thus, in a context in which lynching was

[48] "The Negro Lynchers," *New York Amsterdam News*, August 11, 1934.

TABLE 2. *Percentage of Blacks Lynched by White and Black Mobs in the Delta Region, 1882–1930*

Decade	Black Victim, Black Mob	Black Victim, White Mob	Total Black Victims	Percentage Lynched by Black Mobs	Percentage Lynched by White Mobs
1882–1889	11	37	48	23	77
1890–1899	9	49	58	16	84
1900–1909	11	71	82	13	87
1910–1919	4	42	46	9	91
1920–1930	1	27	28	4	96
Aggregate Total	36	226	262	14	86

Source: Adapted from Project HAL (Historical American Lynching Data Collection Project), http://people.uncw.edu/hinese/HAL/HAL%20Web%20Page.htm (accessed June 3, 2009).

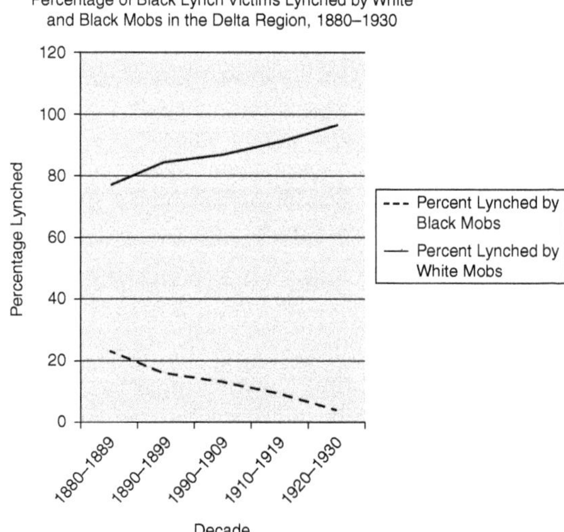

FIGURE 4 Percentage of Black Lynch Victims Lynched by White and Black Mobs in the Delta Region, 1880–1930
Source: Created by author.

viewed as a legitimate response to black criminality, black Americans in general concluded that black vigilantism had to be roundly criticized and discouraged – because to do otherwise might have legitimated the black beast rapist discourse and imperiled the victimization narrative of the lynched black body.

The net result of the racialization of lynching and black-authored narratives condemning black vigilantism is that black Americans increasing eschewed vigilantism after the 1880s. In the South between the years 1882 and 1889, black vigilantism accounted for approximately 10 percent of total lynching incidents. For every subsequent decade, black vigilantism (as a percentage of total lynching incidents) decreased. Similarly, in the Delta region, black vigilante incidents peaked at 23 percent of total lynching episodes during the 1880s and declined every decade thereafter. In addition, 68 percent (or 100 of 148 incidents) of Southern black/integrated vigilante violence and 55 percent (or 20 of 36 incidents) of Delta black vigilantism occurred before 1900. According to historian Terence Finnegan, "Two-thirds of lynching incidents that involved African American participation in mobs [in South Carolina and Mississippi] occurred before 1900 ...," and "after the turn of the century, black-on-black lynchings declined sharply, with only three incidents occurring after 1908."[49] Hence, black vigilantism was primarily a late nineteenth-century phenomenon.[50]

CONCLUSION

By the mid- to late 1880s, lynching had become a racialized phenomenon in which blacks were the primary targets of white lynch mob violence. In addition, the emergent black beast rapist discourse rationalized white-on-black lynching as a moral duty to protect white womanhood. These developments compelled black Americans to increasingly abstain from engaging in or supporting lynching after the 1880s; black extralegal violence may have implied black support for white-on-black lynching and the racist discourses that rationalized it. Therefore, Delta blacks – and by extension black Americans throughout the South – increasingly eschewed lynching, because the negative implications of black vigilantism overwhelmed traditional rationales for it. In Chapter 2, we shall see (1) how

[49] Finnegan, *A Deed So Accursed*, 149–150.
[50] Tolnay and Beck, "When Race Didn't Matter," 136.

African Americans organized resistance to the rising tide of white lynch mob violence in the early twentieth century by mobilizing to prevent lynchings in the making and (2) how antilynching activists fought against the black beast rapist discourse by reframing the lynched black body as a victim of white lynch mob violence.

2

Resisting Lynching

This chapter explores why and how black Americans constructed victimization narratives of the lynched black body in response to the racialization of lynching. Victimization narratives of the lynched black body framed potential and actual black lynch victims as hapless, dehumanized sufferers of white-on-black lynch mob violence. Black-authored victimization narratives of the lynched black body offered a counterpoint to white-authored lynching narratives that framed black lynch victims as black beast rapists or brutes. In response to the latter rhetorical context, black-authored victimization narratives sought to transform how white Americans understood black lynch victims, mobilize black communities and authorities to prevent lynchings in the making, and compel white audiences to support vigorous federal antilynching legislation.

In order to illustrate these themes, this chapter tells the stories of Steve Green's and Henry Lowery's antilynching defense campaigns. Unlike the majority of African Americans whose lives were threatened by white lynch mob violence, in both Green's and Lowery's cases, African American communities beyond the locale of the precipitating event organized vigorous defense campaigns to save the men from all-but-certain lynchings if they were returned to the communities in which their alleged crimes had occurred. The chapter's first section details Steve Green's story. In March 1910, Steve Green, a black tenant farmer, allegedly murdered a white plantation owner, William Sidle, in cold blood in Jericho, Arkansas. Green fled Arkansas with the help of friends and relatives but was later apprehended in Chicago. My analysis of

Steve Green's defense campaign will emphasize how the victimization narrative of the lynched black body compelled Chicago's black community and local authorities to prevent Green's extradition to Arkansas. The chapter's second section analyzes Henry Lowery's story. Approximately ten years after Steve Green's near extradition, in December 1921, Henry Lowery, also a black tenant farmer, was accused of murdering white planter O. T. Craig and his daughter on Christmas Day in Nodena, Arkansas. Like Green, Lowery fled with the aid of black social networks but was later captured by Arkansas authorities in El Paso, Texas. Although Henry Lowery initially alluded Arkansas authorities, he was extradited to Arkansas and lynched upon his return. In response to Henry Lowery's lynching, the NAACP mobilized a national and international publicity campaign aimed at highlighting how white lynch mob violence was brutalizing black Americans. This chapter argues that black-authored victimization narratives of the lynched black body were central to both Steve Green's and Henry Lowery's defense campaigns as well as the NAACP's efforts to convince white Americans to support the passage of a federal antilynching law.

TO SAVE A KINSMEN

Very little is known about Steve Green's background prior to the shooting of William Sidle. According to the *Crisis*, Green was born in Tennessee in 1862. Green never attended school and worked on farms from childhood. At some point, he brought his wife and children to Jericho, Arkansas,[1] probably because of the availability of farm work and its vibrant black community. In the early 1900s, Jericho was a predominantly black unincorporated town that had at least six black merchants, a large school for black children, two black churches, a Masonic hall, and a black-owned funeral home. Most notably, Jack Henry Usher, an African American resident, was one of the town's largest landowners and, for a time, its postmaster and railroad depot agent.[2]

Sometime after Steve Green arrived in Jericho, he began sharecropping for William Sidle. Sidle and his family resided in

[1] "Steve Green's Story," *Crisis: The Record of the Darker Races*, November 1910, 14.

[2] Margaret Elizabeth Woolfolk, *A History of Crittenden County, Arkansas* (Greenville: Southern Historical Press, 1991), 210–213.

nearby Memphis, Tennessee; however, he owned and operated farmland in Jericho. Sidle must have been a large landowner in Jericho, because newspaper reports depicted him as a "rich planter."[3] Not only was Sidle a wealthy planter, but he also married Josephine Clement, one of Crittenden County's first teachers and a descendent of Jericho's founder, Stephen Stonewall. Sidle's apparent wealth and family pedigree likely made him a part of Jericho's white economic and political elite.[4]

On March 2, 1910, Green shot and killed Sidle. Arkansas' white newspapers emphasized that the murder was without cause. The initial *Little Rock Arkansas Gazette* report of the incident noted that Green "was asked to leave" and "negro refused and getting a rifle shoots Sidle through the body."[5] According to the report, Green worked on Sidle's farm; however, Sidle began to have some problems with Green and decided that he would terminate his employment. When Sidle and Sidle's nephew Claude Burnett informed Green of his termination, Green supposedly became enraged and retrieved a Winchester rifle from his home and shot Sidle. In making his escape, Green brandished the rifle in the direction of Burnett until he was a safe distance away. To highlight the fact that Sidle had no ill will toward Green, the report asserted that both Sidle and his nephew had been unarmed because Green had been considered a "peaceable negro" among area whites.[6]

Steve Green told a different story. According to Green, William Sidle decided to raise the land rental fee from five dollars to nine dollars in 1910. In response to the near doubling of the cost of rent, Green recalled that all tenants, including himself, quit or threatened to quit. After Green left the Sidle farm and began working for a nearby farmer, Sidle sent an emissary to warn Green that he would not allow him to work for another farmer in Crittenden County. Apparently, not long after Green had been warned to leave Crittenden County, Sidle spotted Green on a nearby farm and exclaimed, "Didn't I tell you that if you didn't work on my farm that there was not room enough in Crittenden County for you and me to live. I meant just what I said."[7] Green recalled that Sidle drew his pistol and fired three shots that lodged in his neck, left arm,

[3] "Rich Planter Killed by Negro," *Little Rock Arkansas Gazette*, March 3, 1910.
[4] Woolfolk, *A History of Crittenden County, Arkansas*, 210.
[5] "Rich Planter Killed by Negro," *Little Rock Arkansas Gazette*.
[6] Ibid.; "Farmer Killed by Negro," *Osceola Times*, March 10, 1910.
[7] "Steve Green's Story," *Crisis*, 14.

and right leg. Steve Green's and Henry Lowery's stories are rooted in a much broader history of economic relations within the Mississippi-Arkansas Delta region's plantation economy. According to Terence Finnegan, more than 60 percent of all black lynching incidents in Mississippi and South Carolina between 1880 and 1940 involved African American agricultural workers. In the overwhelming majority of lynchings related to agriculture, whites accused tenants of committing a crime against their employer or a member of their employer's immediate family. Murder or assault accounted for more than 50 percent of all crimes that agricultural victims allegedly committed.

Miraculously, after the shooting, Green was able to retreat to his cabin, where he fetched his Winchester rifle, and then returned fire in Sidle's direction. Without knowing whether his bullet had struck Sidle, Green fled the scene of the incident. Within the Mississippi and Arkansas Deltas specifically, black armed self-defense as a response to an anticipated lynching was more often than not precipitated by violent confrontations between blacks and white plantation owners, white merchants, and white police. Approximately 44 percent of black lynch victims were accused of murdering whites between the years 1882 and 1930. If attempted murders are included, over 50 percent of all black lynch victims were accused of murder. The murder of white police and whites connected to the plantation economy represents a significant proportion of the murder allegations, primarily because violence and coercion characterized relations between white authorities, the plantation elite (which included plantation owners, managers/overseers, and merchants), and blacks.[8]

White authorities immediately mobilized a posse to capture Green; however, the search turned up nothing. Green recounted that he was able to initially elude capture because he concealed

[8] See Finnegan, *A Deed So Accursed*, 110–111. In addition, for works that trace the historical development of sharecropping and debt peonage in the South, and particularly Mississippi, see Edward Royce, *The Origins of Southern Sharecropping* (Philadelphia: Temple University Press, 1993); Michael Fitzgerald, "To Give Our Votes to the Party: Black Political Agitation and Agricultural Change in Alabama, 1865–1870," *Journal of American History* 76 (1989): 489–505; Nan Woodruff, *American Congo: The African American Freedom Struggle in the Delta* (Cambridge: Harvard University Press, 2003); Neil R. McMillen, *Dark Journey: Black Mississippians in the Age of Jim Crow* (Urbana: University of Illinois, 1990); and Pete Daniel, *The Shadow of Slavery: Peonage in the South, 1901–1969* (Urbana: University of Illinois Press, 1990).

himself atop a tree until nightfall. Thereafter, Green fled to a nearby town for safe haven. For the next three weeks, Green's friends and relatives provided him with food, money, blankets, and ammunition. Subsequently, Green traveled by foot and rail until he reached Chicago on August 12, 1910.[9]

By August 19, Steve Green was discovered and apprehended by Chicago police. George Chivers, a person whom Green had befriended upon arriving to Chicago, reportedly tipped off Chicago police to Green's whereabouts in exchange for a small bounty. The *Chicago Defender* portrayed Chivers as a "white man's nigger" who betrayed Green because Green had refused to loan him two dollars. The *Defender* also suggested that the black community was so outraged by Chivers's betrayal that his residence was "being watched by enraged young men of the race who have decided to tar and feather him." The newspaper seemingly encouraged black vigilantism for Chivers's betrayal by divulging his home address; however, in the end, the *Defender* asserted that "cooler heads are prevailing on the young man and the chances are they will only invite the brute to leave the city."[10]

After Steve Green's arrest, he recalled that the Chicago police vigorously questioned him about William Sidle's murder. Green initially claimed to be "John Young" and that he knew nothing of the murder. In order to coerce a confession, the Chicago police withheld food and water from Green for several days. As Green's physical condition became dire and his fear of being turned over to Arkansas authorities intensified, he attempted to commit suicide by eating two boxes of matches.[11] Green's attempted suicide reveals that he was willing to die a slow, torturous death by his own hand rather than that of lynchers for a crime he was not sure he had committed. Although his attempted suicide suggested the extent to which he would go to prevent being victimized by white lynch mob violence, his ultimate fate would hinge upon black Chicagoans and white authorities embracing him as an inevitable victim of white lynch mob violence.

Subsequent to Green's attempted suicide, the Chicago police sent for a relative of William Sidle's to identify his shooter. Sidle's relative positively identified Green as the culprit and also taunted

[9] "Steve Green's Story," *Crisis*, 14.

[10] "Chicago Police Gives Colored Man Up to Lynchers," *Chicago Defender*, August 27, 1910.

[11] Ibid.

him that "one thousand people were waiting to burn him in Jericho, Arkansas."[12] With his identity revealed, Green apparently confessed that he had shot at William Sidle but refused to return to Arkansas without extradition papers. In response, the Crittenden County sheriff secured an extradition order from Arkansas governor George Donaghey, who requested that Chicago authorities hold Green until Arkansas authorities arrived with extradition papers.[13]

From a *Chicago Defender* report, antilynching crusader and Chicago resident Ida B. Wells learned that Steve Green had attempted to commit suicide while in Chicago police custody. Wells immediately contacted Chicago's preeminent black attorney, Edward H. Wright, to investigate what could be done to prevent Green's extradition. In the meantime, on August 22, 1910, Governor Donaghey formally requested Illinois governor Charles S. Deneen to release Steve Green into the custody of Arkansas authorities. On the same day, the Illinois governor signed the extradition order. As Steve Green's extradition appeared all but certain, Edward H. Wright served Chicago police authorities with a writ of habeas corpus, which should have forestalled Green's extradition. Wright's plea for a habeas corpus hearing was heard before Judge Tuthill of the Chicago Circuit Court. The contents of Wright's arguments were not discussed in newspaper coverage, nor do extant records of the court proceedings exist. To be sure, convincing a white judge that Green, who was accused of murdering a prominent white planter, should be viewed as a potential victim of white lawlessness rather than as a pariah was likely the chief obstacle in gaining a habeas corpus hearing. Wright likely persuaded Judge Tuthill that the circumstances upon which Green had been arrested and detained in Chicago were suspect enough that he deserved such a hearing. Moreover, Wright likely impressed upon Tuthill that there had been threats to lynch Green upon his return to Arkansas. Whatever Wright's strategy, he successfully convinced Judge Tuthill to convene a habeas corpus proceeding. Yet, rather than complying with the writ, Chicago police released Green into the custody of Arkansas authorities, who promptly told Green "he was the most important Nigger in

12 "Steve Green's Story," *Crisis*, 14.

13 "Seiddle's [*sic*] Slayer May Be Held in Chicago," *Little Rock Arkansas Gazette*, August 19, 1910; "Steve Green Confessed," *Little Rock Arkansas Gazette*, August 21, 1910.

the United States since there was a reception committee of a thousand waiting for him in Arkansas with lighted fire."[14] Green's removal from Chicago police custody and his imminent return to Arkansas ignited a frenzied attempt by Wells and other prominent Chicago blacks to prevent what they believed to be a lynching in the making.

Steve Green's impromptu defense committee worried that once he left Illinois, the court injunction would no longer be valid. In an effort to entice Illinois law enforcement to recapture Green before he got beyond the Illinois border, Wells and Green's attorney convinced the Illinois state attorney to offer a $100 reward for Green's safe return to Chicago. Fortunately, Sheriff Nellis of Alexander County, Illinois, received the attorney's telegram, and, after attaining assurances from Chicago authorities concerning the telegram's validity, Nellis intercepted and apprehended Green in Cairo, Illinois (the southernmost town in the state of Illinois) just as he was about to cross into Missouri. After Green was returned safely to Chicago, Wells praised the Chicago police as exemplary in preventing white mob violence because they "used every method known to modern ingenuity to intercept the prisoner before crossing the line of the State [Illinois]."[15] In the aftermath of Green's dramatic rescue, Wright successfully petitioned Illinois governor Deneen to withhold Green's extradition so that the habeas corpus proceedings could occur.[16]

News reports of Steve Green's amazing rescue elicited widespread interest and support among activist circles within and outside of Chicago. Most notably, wealthy Columbia University professor and benefactor Joel E. Spingarn provided $100 toward Green's defense and promised more if necessary.[17] In addition, several of Chicago's prominent black churches contributed approximately $73 to Green's legal defense fund and private individuals, approximately $8.[18] Beyond financial contributions, the Institutional Church, headed by Archibald J. Carey, who was known as an influential powerbroker in Chicago politics, created a defense committee to

[14] "Steve Green Liberated," *Chicago Defender*, September 24, 1910.
[15] Ibid.
[16] "Chicago Police Gives Colored Man Up to Lynchers," *Chicago Defender*.
[17] Paula Giddings, "Missing in Action: Ida B. Wells, the NAACP, and the Historical Record," *Meridians* 1 (2001): 13.
[18] Personals, *Chicago Defender*, September 3, 1910, and "Great Center of Methodism," *Chicago Defender*, May 6, 1911.

prevent Green's extradition.[19] The committee's first order of business was to hold a mass meeting to brainstorm how to best help Green. According to the *Chicago Defender*, the committee agreed that Green should not be turned over to Arkansas authorities until his case was thoroughly investigated and he was found guilty of the charges lodged against him. In framing a rationale for preventing Steve Green's extradition to Arkansas, black Chicagoans felt compelled to make it clear that they did not support black crime nor aid black fugitives from the law. Archibald Carey declared, "We wish it distinctly understood that we are making no effort to shield Green from just punishment, but we know that he cannot secure a fair trial in Arkansas."[20] To this point, Carey contended that Arkansas authorities' statements that Green would be "the most popular man in Arkansas" provided prima facie evidence that Arkansas authorities would not protect Green from a lynching.[21] Chicago's black community had little faith in police protection and believed that only a significant show of force in the form of a military guard could prevent Green's lynching upon return to Arkansas. Since it was unlikely that Green would receive a military guard for his protection, Chicago's black community banded together to prevent Green's return to Arkansas. Steve Green's habeas corpus hearing records have long been destroyed; therefore, a detailed account of Green's lawyer's arguments, the counterarguments of the state of Illinois, and Judge Tuthill's deliberations cannot be reconstructed. However, what is clear is that Judge Tuthill's ruling seemingly revolved around whether Chicago police violated the circuit court's writ of habeas corpus as well as the soundness of the state of Arkansas' extradition request. During the hearing, Green testified that Sidle shot him four times because he refused to work for him and that in response, Green retrieved his shotgun and shot in Sidle's direction in self-defense. Following Green's testimony, Green's lawyers apparently made the flaws in the state of Arkansas' extradition papers a major point of contention. The *Chicago Defender* humorously reflected that "The Governor of Arkansas could not [be] considered a first-class lawyer, and possibly not one at all" for signing such a poorly

[19] For an in-depth study of Archibald J. Carey and his family, see Dennis C. Dickerson, *African American Preachers and Politics: The Careys of Chicago* (Jackson: University of Mississippi Press, 2010).

[20] "Mass Meeting Aids Fugitive," *Chicago Defender*, September 3, 1910.

[21] Ibid.

constructed extradition order.[22] The state of Arkansas' indictment papers (upon which the extradition was based) contained one significant factual error. Per the *Little Rock Arkansas Gazette*, Steve Green shot and killed William Sidle on March 2, 1910. However, the indictment that accompanied Green's extradition papers claimed that he had "maliciously and feloniously" killed William Sidle on April 10, 1910.[23] Based upon my analysis of the indictment, there were several careless oversights and several crossed-out words (most notably, the indictment initially referred to the current Arkansas governor as Jeff Davis rather than George Donaghey, governor at the time of the incident) that substantiate the *Chicago Defender*'s argument that the extradition request had been poorly developed by Arkansas authorities.

After weighing the arguments of Green's lawyers and the state of Illinois' legal team, Judge Tuthill concluded that the Chicago Police Department had violated the law by releasing Steve Green into the custody of Arkansas authorities, and upon that basis, the judge ruled that Green had to be released from police custody. In response to the verdict, the *Chicago Defender* bristled with excitement. The newspaper exclaimed that the Steve Green case "was the most far-reaching one of its kind in the history of extradition matters before the bar of the State of Illinois" and that it "was one of the greatest legal triumphs of the race, in which first-class black lawyers ably defended and secured victory for a black man accused of murder."[24] In at least this one case, Chicago's black community could celebrate that it had united and then outwitted and outmaneuvered "Judge Lynch" and the system of racial segregation that made it possible.

One week after Green's celebrated release, a mass meeting was held at Chicago's Quinn Chapel. Black leaders and community members showed up en masse to show support and donate additional monies for Steve Green's well-being. Although it was

[22] "Attorneys William G. Anderson and Edward H. Wright Won One of the Greatest Legal Battles of Their Lives," *Chicago Broadax*, September 24, 1910.

[23] Office of the Secretary of State, Executive Section, Requisitions from Other States, 1835–1949, *Requisition of the Governor of Arkansas for Steve Green*, Illinois State Archives, Springfield, Illinois; ibid., Executive Section, Register of Requisitions Issued by Illinois to Other States, 1869–1979, "Steve Green," Illinois State Archives, Springfield, Illinois.

[24] "Attorneys William G. Anderson and Edward H. Wright Won One of the Greatest Legal Battles of Their Lives," *Chicago Broadax*.

initially advertised that Green would tell his story, it was later decided that it was wiser not to permit him to speak, owing to the precariousness of his situation.[25] With the help of Ida B. Wells and others, Green was sneaked out of Chicago; he remained away until Arkansas authorities seemingly gave up trying to arrest him. Green's evasiveness reflected the fact that he remained a fugitive and that consequently new extradition papers could be submitted and Green arrested. Once it appeared safe to return, Green apparently returned to Chicago and slept at the offices of Wells's Negro Fellowship League.[26] Following Green's release from police custody, a *Chicago Defender* editorial advised Green to quietly change his name and relocate to a new town where he could live undetected.[27] This was wise advice, given that in January 1911, the governor of Arkansas reinstated a $200 reward for Green's arrest.[28]

Whether Steve Green remained in Chicago under an assumed identity is unclear. Whatever shape Green's life took post hearing, the legacy of his miraculous escape made a deep and lasting imprint on black Americans in Chicago and beyond. For example, Green's case was credited with causing future NAACP president Joel Spingarn to help bankroll the organization's early campaigns against lynching.[29] In the years following the trial, during the men's respective campaigns for political office, the *Chicago Defender* routinely argued that attorney E. H. Wright's and community leader Archibald Carey's handling of the Green case illustrated their selfless character and credentials as bona fide race leaders.[30] In addition, Ida B. Wells used Steve Green's story as a means to further galvanize antilynching activism in Chicago's black community. In a 1911 speech before black churchgoers, Wells emphasized that Chicago was a citadel from which a full-fledged assault on lynching could be prosecuted. In order to reinforce this point, Wells declared that

[25] Editorial, *Chicago Defender*, October 8, 1910.

[26] Wells and Duster, *Crusade for Justice*, 337.

[27] Editorial, *Chicago Defender*, October 8, 1910.

[28] "Reinstates Reward for Steve Green," *Little Rock Arkansas Gazette*, January 17, 1911.

[29] Giddings, "Missing in Action," 13–14; "Hold Private Funeral for Col. J. E. Spingarn," *Chicago Defender*, August 5, 1939.

[30] "Great Center of Methodism," *Chicago Defender*, May 6, 1911; "In the Political World," *Chicago Defender*, February 24, 1912; "Hon. E. H. Wright Passes on Bonds for Windy City," February 24, 1912; and "Jack Johnson Wins Abduction Suit – L. Cameron Would Not Appear against Him," *Chicago Defender*, August 21, 1915.

without mass meetings and community involvement in Chicago, Steve Green would have been lynched. For Wells, it was important for black Chicagoans to understand the ways in which they bore responsibility for Green's release, because it suggested that they bore responsibility for hundreds of other black men and women who were victims of lynch mob violence in other locales.[31]

Steve Green's defense campaign sought to convince white authorities that if they did not aid in preventing Green's extradition or guarantee him a fair trial upon his return to Arkansas, he would be an inevitable victim of white lynch mob violence. By stressing to Illinois governor Deneen and Judge Tuthill that William Sidle's nephew and Arkansas authorities had told Green that he would be lynched once he was extradited to Arkansas, black Chicagoans – and especially attorney E. H. Wright and Ida B. Wells – employed the victimization narrative of the lynched black body to successfully help forestall Green's appointed fate. As we shall see, Steve Green's improbable triumph appears all the more so when considered in comparison with Henry Lowery's defense campaign.

AN AMERICAN LYNCHING

Details about the identities of Henry Lowery and O. T. Craig were scantily reported in newspaper coverage following Craig's alleged murder and Lowery's lynching. However, certain details can be established. According to regional and national news dailies, O. T. Craig was a seventy-year-old wealthy planter who owned a large plantation in Mississippi County, Arkansas, near to Memphis, Tennessee. Both of Craig's two sons oversaw plantation affairs, and his son Richard (known as "Mr. Dick") was reported to have had a bad reputation among black laborers. In Mississippi County, the Craig family was revered as "one of the best known and most respected families in Northeast Arkansas." Henry Lowery, accompanied by his wife and daughter, began working for the Craig family approximately two years prior to the fatal confrontation. Following Craig's death, regional white dailies portrayed Henry Lowery as a man of "bad character" who owned a whiskey still and had been arrested several times for petty crimes.[32]

[31] "The North Side Society," *Chicago Defender*, June 17, 1911.

[32] "Negro Kills Planter and His Daughter," *Little Rock Arkansas Gazette*, December 26, 1920.

White and black newspaper narratives about the Craig killings differed dramatically. In general, white newspapers portrayed Lowery as drunk when he arrived at the Craig plantation. For example, white newspapers reported that the confrontation between Craig and Lowery was initiated by Lowery's abuse of a black female employee on the Craig plantation. Reportedly, she plead for the Craigs to protect her from Lowery's drunken rage. When Craig intervened to break up the dispute, Lowery wantonly shot him. This widely reported narrative precluded the possibility that Lowery and Craig's altercation could have occurred in response to interpersonal antagonisms precipitated by the exploitative relations of the plantation economy. White newspapers subtly inverted the familiar black beast rapist narrative, in which the narrative's damsel in distress was a cherished "black cook" who was assaulted by the stereotypically depraved and uncontrollable black beast. Thus, O. T. Craig courageously intervened to prevent the assault of one of his female employees, and, as in the traditional narrative, Craig's motivation was to defend feminine honor. The totality of white newspaper coverage, then, presented Henry Lowery as a "black fiend" who deserved to be lynched.[33] Furthermore, by portraying Lowery as armed and dangerous, white newspapers insinuated that Lowery had to be lynched.

Police and local residents immediately organized a search posse and offered a $1,000 reward for Lowery's arrest. The reward advertisement emphasized that Lowery was wanted dead or alive. From the beginning, police suspected that Lowery was securing food and shelter from local blacks, a belief that in turn led police to search the homes of Lowery's friends and family. A few miles from the Craig plantation, Lowery was temporarily surrounded by police, but he was able to elude them by fleeing into a nearby swamp. After this close call, Lowery was able to outwit and evade police authorities until his capture and arrest in El Paso, Texas.[34]

In the aftermath of Lowery's lynching, the NAACP sent national field secretary William Pickens to Memphis to investigate. Pickens talked with numerous locals and subsequently wrote a thorough report for the national office and penned "American Congo,"

33 "Negro Slayer Burned at the Stake," *Little Rock Arkansas Gazette*, January 27, 1921.

34 "Negro Slayer May Be Captured Soon," *Little Rock Arkansas Gazette*, December 29, 1920; "$1,000 Reward," *Osceola Times*, January 7, 1921; "Search for Negro Wanted at Wilson," *Little Rock Arkansas Gazette*, January 9, 1921.

a scathing exposé of the lynching that was published in major black newspapers. Whereas white newspapers portrayed Lowery as a black fiend, William Pickens's investigation revealed that Lowery was reputed as honest, hardworking, well behaved, and industrious among his fellow laborers on the Craig plantation. Pickens's report to the NAACP as well as his "American Congo" essay maintained that a dispute over "settlement" precipitated the violent altercation between Henry Lowery and O. T. Craig. Within the plantation economy, asking for a payment settlement was considered a subversive act that directly threatened the facade of debt upon which sharecropping was premised. Craig not only refused to "settle up" but also violently assaulted Lowery for presuming to dictate terms. On Christmas Day, Lowery returned to the Craig plantation to press for a settlement. As before, Craig reportedly struck Lowery over the head for his seeming insubordination. According to Pickens, fearing for his life, Lowery fled from the Craig plantation, but not before O. T. Craig's son Richard shot him. Details about what occurred next are less clear, save to say that Lowery returned fire, killing O. T. Craig and his daughter and severely wounding his two sons.[35]

On January 19, Henry Lowery was captured in El Paso, Texas, after Arkansas authorities intercepted a letter written by him. The letter was addressed to Morris Jenkins, a fraternal lodge member, whom Lowery had instructed to go in person and make inquires of J. T. Williamson, another fraternal lodge member, concerning the whereabouts of his wife and child. Instead, Jenkins wrote a letter to Williamson, which was subsequently intercepted by police authorities. Beyond asking for information regarding his family, Lowery had relayed his plans for escaping to Mexico and, most damaging, revealed his location. The *Memphis Press* gained access to Lowery's letter and reprinted a portion of its contents. Lowery reportedly wrote,

> It affords me no small pleasure to write you a few lines to let you hear from me. This leaves me very well in health and I truly hope these few lines will find you and family well and doing well. Listen, I have made it to the border line, but I have not crossed yet. I have run out of money and am trying to get me a job to work some. Soon as I get money enough I am going over in Mexico. It costs me $10 to cross over. Have you heard from my wife and girl

[35] "The American Congo – the Burning of Henry Lowery," *Philadelphia Tribune*, March 26, 1921.

or Williams? Write now and tell me all you know about the matter. Now I can't see nothing in the paper here where I am at. I am over a thousand miles from you now and as soon as I get some more money I am going further. I am now in El Paso, Texas right on the border, so you write me at once and let me hear how is everything.[36]

To a certain degree, it is shocking that Lowery would give away his position in his letter to friends and family in Arkansas or even decide to send a letter to Arkansas. Given the intense manhunt for Lowery and the substantial reward for his arrest, Lowery certainly would have known that any letter intercepted by whites would have necessarily put in danger those to whom the letter was addressed. However, because he had to leave his wife and child behind, Lowery likely felt compelled to make sure that they were not in harm's way even though sending them a letter would exacerbate that possibility.

Once in custody, Arkansas authorities requested that El Paso officials hold Lowery until he could be questioned by them. According to newspaper reports, El Paso police apprehended Lowery without resistance at an office building in downtown El Paso.[37] Lowery confessed that while he was on the run, he had adopted the alias "Sam Turrell." Moreover, Lowery reportedly relayed to El Paso police authorities the story of his escape from Arkansas. Lowery recalled,

When the mob formed and took after me I ran and hid in the brush till after dark. Then I began crawling and crawled until morning. Lots of times men in the posse were near me and once they nearly stepped on me. It was cold and much of the time I had to crawl through mud and water.[38]

After that, Lowery secretly boarded a train and made his way to Dallas, and from there to El Paso, Texas. After divulging the details of his escape, Lowery reportedly pleaded with the El Paso police to kill him or allow him to commit suicide. Almost prophetically, Lowery was reported to have stated, "If they ever get me back to Turrell, they'll burn me and never give me a trial. I know it boss. For God's sake, shoot me now or give me a razor and I'll do it myself. I'll never be a day in jail at Turrell before I'm burned at the

[36] "Anxiety to Hear from Home Cause of Negro's Death," *Memphis Press*, January 27, 1921.

[37] "Negro Killed White Man and Daughter on Christmas Day, Officers Say; Arrested Here," *El Paso Times*, January 25, 1921.

[38] Ibid.

stake."[39] As Lowery's quote suggests, he was in a state of panic once he was arrested and jailed in El Paso. In his mind, El Paso authorities were the only thing standing between him and a lynch mob. The fact that Lowery preferred suicide is not surprising, particularly given the brutality he likely imagined would be exacted upon his body during a lynching. As with Steve Green, the specter of the lynched black body so haunted Lowery that in a moment of weakness, he desired a self-appointed death rather than an imposed one. (In Chapter 3, we shall see how black writers elevated to a heroic status fictional black lynch victims who seemingly chose how they would die.)

On January 20, the day after Lowery's arrest and interrogation, his lawyer, Fred C. Knollenberg, negotiated the terms of Lowery's release to Arkansas authorities with Arkansas governor Thomas McRae. Knollenberg proposed to waive an extradition proceeding in exchange for Lowery being held at the Arkansas State Penitentiary with police protection until his trial. Perhaps Lowery and his lawyer believed he would inevitably be returned to Arkansas; in that case, resisting extradition proceedings would simply prolong the inevitable. As Knollenberg negotiated with Governor McRae, he sent a telegram to the governor of Texas asking that he be notified if the state of Arkansas initiated extradition proceedings. Per Knollenberg's telegram, he intended to block extradition if the governor of Arkansas refused to guarantee police protection for Lowery. In the meantime, the El Paso branch of the NAACP entreated the president of the National Baptist Convention to appeal for protection directly to Governor McRae on Lowery's behalf. After a spate of telegrams, Governor McRae agreed to hold Lowery in the state penitentiary until the trial. However, white newspapers reported that Arkansas authorities disembarked with Lowery before receiving the governor's instructions that the prisoner was to be taken to the state penitentiary for safekeeping.[40] On January 23, Governor McRae sent a frantic telegram to Knollenberg stating, "Your message

39 "Lowery, in Jail, Asks Police to Kill Him," *Memphis Commercial Appeal*, January 20, 1921; "Lowery, Negro Murder Captured in El Paso, Texas," *Osceola Times*, January 21, 1921.

40 "Will Bring Negro Back to Arkansas," *Little Rock Arkansas Gazette*, January 23, 1921; "Alleged Slayer to Be Held at Wales," *Little Rock Arkansas Gazette*, January 24, 1921; Robert Zangrando, ed., Papers of the NAACP, Part 7: *The Anti-Lynching Campaign, 1912–1955, Series A: Anti-Lynching Investigative Files,*

received late, if officers have left there with Lowery please intercept their train with message to deliver Lowery to Arkansas penitentiary."[41] In addition, the governor of Texas assisted by empowering Texas police to detain Lowery if spotted. By January 25, the *El Paso Times* reported that Governor McRae's order that Arkansas authorities take Lowery directly to Little Rock had been conveyed.[42]

Contrary to established protocol, Arkansas deputies blatantly violated Governor McRae's orders to take Lowery directly to Little Rock. Instead, they took a circuitous route that began in El Paso, then went to New Orleans, and then to a train station in Sardis, Mississippi. The most direct route from El Paso to Little Rock would have taken Lowery through Dallas and Texarkana, Texas, rather than New Orleans. The actual route might be explained by authorities' desire to travel an unanticipated way that would likely circumvent any efforts to rescue Lowery. This roundabout route also suggests that Arkansas authorities more than likely colluded with mob leaders, establishing the Sardis train station as the prearranged rendezvous point for handing over Lowery to them. In fact, approximately thirty minutes before the train carrying Lowery arrived at the Sardis station, a mob of fifteen to twenty men was waiting for its arrival in a hotel lobby. As the men waited for the train to arrive, one of the mob leaders admitted that they had received information that Lowery would be traveling from New Orleans aboard an Illinois Central train scheduled to arrive in Sardis at 5:30 a.m. When the train pulled into Sardis, the men reportedly drew their weapons, boarded the train, and seized Lowery without any resistance from either the Arkansas deputy or the on-duty train marshal.[43]

Even though the mob's capture of Lowery was highly publicized, Lowery's executors seemingly did not fear interference from police authorities. Brazenly, the mob reportedly stopped to purchase rope

1912–1953 (Frederick: University Publications of America, 1987), reel 2, frames 0791–0845.

[41] Zangrando, Papers of the NAACP, reel 2, frames 0791–0845.

[42] "Negro Killed White Man and Daughter on Christmas Day, Officers Say; Arrested Here," *El Paso Times*.

[43] "Governor Would Avert Lynching," *Little Rock Arkansas Gazette*, January 25, 1921; "How Mob Took Negro From the Train at Sardis," *Memphis Press*, January 26, 1921; "The American Congo – the Burning of Henry Lowery," *Philadelphia Tribune*, March 26, 1921.

and to have lunch in Millington, Tennessee, prior to returning Lowery to the spot of the alleged crime. In part, mob participants could take comfort in the fact that police authorities were first and foremost white men who understood that the maintenance of white supremacy demanded a violent reprisal. Doing their part as honorable white men meant that police officers would conspicuously conclude that Lowery was killed "at the hands of persons unknown." For instance, even though mob leaders reportedly chatted with the railroad marshal in Sardis and wore no masks to conceal their identities, the Arkansas officers tasked with shepherding Lowery to the state penitentiary stated that they could neither ascertain their identities nor recognize any mob members. Moreover, Arkansas deputies even disputed the idea that the mob members could have been from Arkansas.[44]

On January 26, approximately one month after fleeing the Arkansas Delta, Henry Lowery was burned to death in Nodena, Arkansas. White newspapers (particularly those from Arkansas and Tennessee) focused the white reader's gaze on how Henry Lowery's life was slowly and painfully extinguished. According to these reports, "scores of curiosity seekers," three hundred to five hundred people, arrived from various towns and cities in the vicinity to witness Lowery's lynching. The reports also stated that the mob treated Lowery kindly; they allowed him to speak with his wife and child and provided him a hearty meal. Afterward, Lowery was chained to a large wooden log, and a pyre was assembled around his feet. Then Lowery's body and the pyre were soaked in gasoline before a fire was started. Reports emphasized that Lowery's body burned for thirty or forty minutes before he died. Apparently, as Lowery's body was burning, he attempted to inhale smoke from the fire to hasten his death, but a mob participant intervened to prevent this. These details were likely added to demonstrate that no mercy was shown Lowery and that hence he was made to suffer to the fullest extent possible. For instance, the *El Paso Times* reported that while Lowery's body burned, his cries of agony could be heard upward of a mile away. Interestingly, white regional papers such as the *Memphis Press* asserted that Lowery did not beg for mercy even though he experienced unimaginable suffering. Rather, it was

44 "Arkansas Negro Seized on Train at Sardis, Miss.," *Memphis News Scimitar*, January 26, 1921; "Wild Rumors of Mob Parade Put Edgar in Action," *Memphis New Scimitar*, January 26, 1921.

reported that Lowery met death bravely and only whimpered slightly as the flames slowly engulfed and roasted his body. By mentioning that Lowery remained quiet, the news reports were not likely attempting to enhance Lowery's manliness, but rather suggesting that Lowery's lack of protest in his final moments signified his guilty resignation. Lowery's gruesome death as depicted in regional newspapers was meant to satiate aggrieved whites' appetite for revenge as well as restore collective confidence in white mastery over black bodies.[45]

In contrast to celebratory depictions, black newspapers characterized white newspaper coverage of the Henry Lowery lynching as "lies of the associated press" because of their willful distortion of the events that precipitated the violent encounter between Lowery and the Craigs.[46] The *Baltimore African American* cited William Pickens's "American Congo" as evidence that various white newspapers fabricated the circumstances surrounding the Lowery-Craig confrontation. Moreover, black newspapers decried the fact that Lowery's lynching would not have been possible without police complicity. The *Chicago Defender* asserted that the identities of the men who committed the lynching were well known and that Arkansas authorities were complicit in Lowery's lynching because they handed him over to the mob without resistance. More damning, other black newspapers stressed that the time and place of Lowery's lynching was announced in advance, yet police authorities did nothing to prevent it. In highlighting local complicity in the lynching, black newspapers articulated why lynching should be considered a federal crime and prosecuted at the federal level; without this deterrent, they argued, the lynching of black bodies would remain "America's national pastime."[47]

It should be noted that it was the practice of black newspapers to reprint excerpts from white newspapers' coverage, which was bracketed with bits of commentary in order to "convict" lynchers using the assumed unbiased testimony of white reporters. Within

[45] "Negro Slayer Burned at the Stake," *Little Rock Arkansas Gazette*, January 27, 1921; "Oil Soaked Body of Henry Lowery Burns 40 Minutes," *El Paso Times*, January 27, 1921; "Hundreds Gather to Watch Lynchers Carry Out Their Grewsome [*sic*] Death Sentence," *Memphis Press*, January 27, 1921.

[46] "Lies of the Associated Press," *Baltimore Afro-American*, March 25, 1921.

[47] "America's Favorite Pastime," *Baltimore Afro-American*, February 4, 1921; "Gasoline and Dry Leaves Used by Whites," *Chicago Defender*, February 5, 1921.

this framework, black newspapers' selections typically emphasized white depravity and particularly the extent to which the white mob reveled in a lynch victim's suffering. A key aim of black newspapers in doing this was to debunk the idea that white mobs enacted civilized punishment on deviant black bodies. For instance, the *Chicago Defender* depicted white mob members as cannibals who feverishly feasted on Lowery's burned flesh. Particular attention was focused on white newspaper accounts of how the mob took pains to slowly "roast" Lowery "inch by inch" and how some white spectators who were anxious to mutilate his body even "bit him in the side with their teeth and then cut out the flesh with pocket knives." Even more macabre, "Lowery's eyes were punched out by a schoolboy who begged to 'take a shot' at the nigger."[48] As these quotations suggest, like white newspaper accounts of white-on-black lynching, black news reports of lynching could engage in hyperbole. This practice reflected the culture of sensationalistic journalism and the language of scandal that was prevalent at the time.[49] On a deeper level, black newspapers' embellishments of white brutality reflected their desire to make the pain and suffering of black lynch victims as compelling as possible.

As stated earlier, white newspapers, such as the *Memphis Commercial Appeal*, reported that Lowery remained silent throughout the lynching. This seemingly minor detail was seized upon in black newspaper coverage. When black newspapers emphasized that Henry Lowery did not whimper or beg for mercy, they suggested that victory over the lynched black body had not been complete; therefore, white lynchers and spectators had been deprived of their chief objective. Given the immense pain Lowery endured, if he had been guilty, black newspaper reports suggested, he would have confessed to the crime in an effort to appeal for mercy. However, in Lowery's distress, he reportedly confessed that several members of his fraternal lodge assisted him in escaping to Texas. Despite this admission, black newspapers presented Lowery as an innocent man who was wrongly put to death. More importantly, despite his innocence, Lowery was not cowardly at the moment of death, but rather faced death with courage and resolve. In this way, Lowery could be presented as illustrating

48 "Gasoline and Dry Leaves Used by Whites," *Chicago Defender*.

49 For a detailed and nuanced discussion of narrative and journalistic practices at the turn of the century, see Lisa Duggan, *Sapphic Slashers: Sex, Violence, and American Modernity* (Durham: Duke University Press, 2000), 35.

black humanity in the face of white depravity. As we shall see in Chapter 3, this rhetorical strategy would become a central motif for black writers seeking to reinscribe black subjectivity in a broader effort to construct consoling narratives of the lynched black body.[50]

As if the lynching of Henry Lowery had not been enough to quench white lynchers' lust for retribution, white vigilantes promised that Lowery's accomplices would be lynched as well. The desired targets were five blacks who had been jailed in Crittenden County for allegedly aiding and abetting Lowery. Morris Jenkins (whom Lowery had written to ascertain the whereabouts of his family) and his wife were accused of providing shelter to Lowery. In addition, three officers in the Odd Fellows lodge were charged with raising funds to help Lowery escape to El Paso, Texas.[51] The lynch mobs' threats were not unprecedented; the consequences of aiding black fugitives were usually deadly. For instance, in the 1906 near lynching of Nathan McDaniels in Clarksdale, Mississippi, McDaniels narrowly escaped because Hiram McDaniels, his brother, facilitated his escape by providing him a mule. When it became clear that Nathan McDaniels had escaped, the mob gathered outside the Clarksdale train depot and lynched Hiram McDaniels after he confessed to police that he had assisted in his brother's escape.[52] Thus, amid persistent reports of an attack on the jail in which Lowery's alleged accomplices were being

[50] "America's Favorite Pastime," *Baltimore Afro-American*; "Gasoline and Dry Leaves Used by Whites," *Chicago Defender*; "Lies of the Associated Press," *Baltimore Afro-American*.

[51] "Six Crittenden County Negroes Brought Here," *Little Rock Arkansas Gazette*, January 29, 1921; see John M. Giggie, *After Redemption: Jim Crow and the Transformation of African American Religion in the Delta, 1875–1915* (New York: Oxford University Press, 2007), 63. According to historian John Giggie, the Odd Fellows Lodge, the largest and most popular black fraternal organization in the Mississippi-Arkansas Delta, boasted 117,505 members by 1901. The growth in fraternal lodges occurred in response to new railroad lines, which made recruitment efforts easier. More importantly, black males believed that fraternal associations offered alternative avenues for asserting dignity and status. In addition, fraternal lodges offered black males a measure of financial and emotional stability that was otherwise impossible during Jim Crow. For instance, fraternal lodges offered burial and sickness insurance and small loans for business development and home purchases. Based upon these overlapping and dense social ties, black fraternal members would have risked their lives to help secure safe passage of potential lynch victims when possible.

[52] "Near Lynching at Clarksdale," *Memphis Commercial Appeal*, September 5, 1909.

held, they were sneaked out of Arkansas and ultimately placed in police custody in Little Rock, Arkansas.[53] It appears that the alleged accomplices escaped lynching, but it is unclear if they were prosecuted for aiding and abetting Henry Lowery's escape.

In the days following the Lowery lynching, Arkansas governor Thomas McRae repeatedly denounced it. McRae angrily declared that "the lynching of Henry Lowery, negro at Nodena, Ark. was the most disreputable and inexcusable act ever committed in Arkansas and declared that he would recommend to the legislature that any sheriff or officer who permits or does not prevent the lynching of a person within his jurisdiction be summarily removed from office." Governor McRae's comments were motivated by the fact that "officers apparently turned him over to a mob in Mississippi with lamb-like docility and permitted his transportation across the Mississippi river into Arkansas and his burning at the stake without any effort to prevent his execution by mob violence."[54] McRae went a step further by adding,

> Inasmuch as the negro was taken from an interstate train and brought from Mississippi into Arkansas where he was killed, the matter may come within the purview of federal authorities, and it is possible that this occurrence may result in the enactment of federal statutes for the prevention of crimes which should be prevented by our county officers.[55]

It is interesting to note that, ten years earlier, the state had passed "An Act to prevent Mob Violence and Lynching within the state of Arkansas."[56] Although it was an antilynching measure on its face, this law simply devised a legal framework for arranging a speedy trial for an alleged black rapist or murderer and fines for sheriffs who failed to notify a circuit judge of an anticipated lynching. No provisions were made to criminalize lynching. Given Arkansas' relatively weak antilynching statues and the fact that Southern governors typically disapproved of federalism, the NAACP greeted McRae's seeming endorsement of a federal antilynching law with

[53] "Nodena Negroes in Little Rock Pen for Safety," *Memphis News Scimitar*, January 28, 1921; "Ark Negroes Go from Memphis to Little Rock Pen," *Memphis Press*, January 26, 1921.

[54] "Governor Irate at Lynching Negro," *Little Rock Arkansas Gazette*, January 27, 1921; "Governor Again Scores Lynchers," *Little Rock Arkansas Gazette*, January 28, 1921.

[55] "Governor Irate at Lynching Negro," *Little Rock Arkansas Gazette*.

[56] Acts of Arkansas, 1819–1976, reel 8, frames 776–778, Arkansas History Commission, Little Rock, Arkansas.

praise. The Arkansas governor's criticism of police authorities lent credence to the NAACP's claim that federal rather than state power was needed to remedy mob violence. In response, the NAACP sent a telegram to the Arkansas governor, extolling him for his stance on Lowery's lynching as well as admonishing him to prevent any further violence against Lowery's alleged accomplices.[57]

As the Arkansas political establishment pursued damage control, the NAACP secretly sent William Pickens to Arkansas to investigate Lowery's lynching. Pickens reported that Arkansas blacks, even those in urban areas such as Little Rock, were frightened to share information about the lynching. Despite the climate of fear among blacks in Arkansas, Pickens gathered important details about Lowery and his lynching that would enable the organization to develop a national and international antilynching publicity campaign in pursuit of a federal antilynching law. The NAACP had been actively lobbying Congress to legislate against lynching since 1918. In the process, they came to realize that publicizing lynchings was their best weapon against the practice.[58] Seeking to take full advantage of white newspapers' complicity in Lowery's lynching as well as their gratuitous depictions of Lowery's torture, the NAACP reproduced facsimile copies of the newspapers' celebratory coverage in the country's most widely circulated black newspapers in order to embarrass American politicians who were reticent about a federal antilynching law.[59]

Beginning in late February 1921, the NAACP ratcheted up their publicity campaign by compiling the most sensational white newspaper reports of the Henry Lowery lynching (mostly from the *Memphis Free Press* and the *Memphis Scimitar*) into an eight-page pamphlet entitled "An American Lynching." According to the organization's records, it sent out more than ten thousand copies of the pamphlet to news organizations in the United States and abroad. In the press kit sent to American and international newspapers, the NAACP emphasized that "An American Lynching" contained facsimile copies of news reports of the Henry

[57] Zangrando, Papers of the NAACP, reel 2, frames 0791–0845.

[58] See Zangrando, *The NAACP Crusade against Lynching*, 38; for an up-to-date and comprehensive narrative history of the NAACP, see Gilbert Jonas, *Freedom's Sword: The NAACP and the Struggle against Racism in America, 1909–1969* (New York: Routledge, 2005).

[59] For example, see *Baltimore Afro-American*, February 25, 1921.

Lowery lynching with "no commentary" from the NAACP.[60] The no commentary assertion belied the carefully crafted letter to newspaper editors and, more importantly, the careful selection of news reports that the organization believed would powerfully convey the brutality of white mob violence, the depth of black victimization, and the bewildering scope of Southern state authorities' negligence. In this sense, "An American Lynching" emphatically commented upon the Henry Lowery lynching without the presence of an identifiable narrator. However, as a rhetorical ploy, the NAACP's no commentary assertion was a brilliantly hatched public relations scheme, because it urged white readers to embrace the pamphlet's veracity based upon the fact that its content had been corroborated and reported by Southern white newspapers. The assumption here is that black voices or black perspectives might have been viewed as partial, and therefore the accuracy of the information regarded as questionable. Also, if the goal was to influence the hearts and minds of Northern whites or nonblack audiences more broadly, it seems that the NAACP calculated that only white testimony about black lynch victims could make black suffering real. By capturing the story of Henry Lowery's burning as told by white newspapers, the NAACP sought to convict Southern whites with their own words and imply that American newspapers, the American public, and American police authorities stood by idly while Henry Lowery's burning at the stake was planned, publicized, and prosecuted. By framing the Lowery lynching as an "American" lynching, the NAACP sought to implicate all Americans in the story.

Much like a lynching photograph that provided irrefutable evidence that white-on-black violence had occurred, the NAACP calculated that white Southern newspapers' graphic depictions of the Henry Lowery lynching would effectively and unproblematically convey white barbarity and black victimization. The NAACP's construction of a victimization narrative of the lynched black body in "An American Lynching" centered upon making an explicit connection between black victimization and local authorities' negligence and lax attitude toward preventing white-on-black lynching. For instance, the pamphlet reprinted the *Memphis Press*'s news reports with the headlines "Lynching Party on Way to Ark. To Pass thru Memphis" and "Avengers Set 6 O'clock as

[60] Zangrando, Papers of the NAACP, reel 2, frames 0791–0845.

Lynching Hour." These articles detailed how lynch mob leaders had planned to parade Henry Lowery through the streets of Memphis. After removing Lowery from police custody in Sardis, Mississippi, a mob leader purportedly declared, "We are going to parade him thru Main st. when we pass thru Memphis.... Then we are going to take him to Arkansas, and that will be the end of him."[61] However, at the last minute, the plan was scuttled because Memphis police had blocked all roads into the city in anticipation of the parade. Lowery's captors (with Lowery in tow) then decided to stop and have lunch at a restaurant on the outskirts of Memphis before continuing on to the alleged murder scene where Lowery was to be lynched at 6 o'clock. The NAACP likely hoped that the above-mentioned news reports conveyed how Lowery's lynchers were unafraid of being identified and that, as a result, they carried out a premeditated and publicly orchestrated lynching in which local authorities failed to prevent or subsequently arrest and prosecute participants. In fact, despite the time and location of Henry Lowery's lynching being published in both local and regional newspapers in advance, local authorities argued that they were helpless to prevent the brutal murder. Sheriff Dwight H. Blackwood, who had been responsible for delivering Henry Lowery to the Arkansas Penitentiary, stated in an article included in "An American Lynching" that "Nearly every man, woman, and child wanted the negro lynched. When public sentiment is that way, there isn't much chance left for the officers." Interestingly, Arkansas governor Thomas McRae reportedly phoned Sheriff Blackwood about sending state troops to Nodena in order to prevent the threatened lynching. However, according to reports, the sheriff was unavailable to take the call and never requested that the governor send state troops.[62] In this way, the NAACP's "An American Lynching" (1) underscored how local authorities' willful negligence and lax approach to preventing and punishing lynching created a context in which white lynch mobs believed they could lynch black Americans with impunity and (2) suggested that black victimization would continue unabated unless federal intervention occurred.

Within this context of legal impunity for those who participated in white-on-black lynching, "An American Lynching" emphasized

[61] Ibid.
[62] Ibid.

how white lynchers enacted horrific and inhumane torture rituals upon black bodies. Whereas black newspapers and some white newspapers discussed Lowery's identity and the ways in which Lowery sought to save himself from lynching and preserve a measure of dignity in the final moments of his life, the NAACP's victimization narrative emphasized how Lowery was dehumanized. For example, one reprinted article from the *Memphis Press* stated,

> Inch by inch the negro was fairly cooked to death. Every few minutes fresh leaves were tossed on the funeral pyre until the blaze had passed the negro's waist. As the flames were eating away his abdomen, a member of the mob stepped forward and saturated the body with gasoline. It was then only a few minutes until the negro had been reduced to ashes.[63]

Following this passage, the article declared, "Words fail to describe the suffering of the negro."[64] The NAACP hoped that such descriptions would illustrate that white-on-black lynch mob violence went far beyond executing black victims for alleged criminality. Rather, white lynchers enacted inhuman torture rituals upon helpless blacks whom the white police and white court of the South either refused or were unable to protect. From the NAACP's perspective, in order to elicit sympathy from white Americans, black lynch victims had to be "perfect" victims who lacked any effective means to respond to their victimization. In fact, the NAACP only aggressively publicized lynching cases in which the victims could be understood as perfect victims of white racial violence, because lynch victims who fought back or had character shortcomings might not elicit white sympathy and, even worse, might embarrass the organization.[65] Thus, details of Lowery's identity and stoic defiance were suppressed in "An American Lynching." Furthermore, the pamphlet cynically framed Lowery as a perfect victim because the NAACP calculated that white shame could be maximized only if whites believed that their actions and their actions alone were responsible for lynching and that only their actions could bring an end to lynching.

Besides these considerations, in crafting "An American Lynching," the NAACP had to deal with the reality that black life

[63] Ibid.

[64] Ibid.

[65] For a more elaborate explanation of the NAACP's selection of cases to publicize for its federal antilynching law campaign, see Kidada E. Williams, *They Left Great Marks on Me*, 189–191.

was far removed from the daily experience of most whites. For progressive and sympathetic whites in the United States and people abroad, black lynch victims could temporarily be embraced as an object of pity but easily discarded as the South's problem. According to historian Khalil Muhammad, "A much graver problem for the NAACP was that for white Americans of every stripe – from radical southern racists to northern progressives – African American criminality became one of the most widely accepted bases for justifying prejudicial thinking, discriminatory treatment, and/or acceptance of racial violence as an instrument of public safety."[66] Therefore, in order to effectively bring attention to black victimization and provoke white sympathy, the NAACP believed that it had to demonstrate how white Americans were damaged by lynching. Therefore, in framing Henry Lowery's lynching as an "American lynching" as well as an "American shame," the NAACP implicitly suggested that it was not simply the burning of Henry Lowery that was of concern, but rather it was the souls of whites and white civilization that needed to be brought into question.

Within weeks of forwarding the "An American Lynching" pamphlet to editors and newspapers throughout South America, Europe, and Asia, letters of support from those institutions began to pour in. The NAACP had counted upon this response. In addition to the pamphlet, the organization attached a cover letter that prompted targeted newspapers "to comment on the phases of American civilization which this publication reveals." It followed this prompt with the statement "If you are moved to protest against conditions which make such occurrences possible, we shall be glad to publish what you may have to say to the American people."[67] In encouraging newspaper editors to write editorials or feature stories condemning the Lowery lynching, the NAACP hoped to move national public opinion toward embracing a federal antilynching law. The organization likely hoped that in galvanizing antilynching sentiment abroad, the international editors would in turn put pressure upon their governments to condemn American lynchings. The strategy appeared to work.

[66] Khalil Gibran Muhammad, *The Condemnation of Blackness: Race, Crime, and the Making of Modern Urban America* (Cambridge: Harvard University Press, 2010), 4; for a broader discussion of how blackness became equated with criminality at the turn of the twentieth century, see chapter 2.

[67] Zangrando, Papers of the NAACP, reel 2, frames 0791–0845.

American newspapers such as the *New York Nation* and the *Boston Evening News* ran editorials or feature stories condemning the lynching. Internationally, several British newspaper editors responded favorably to the NAACP's query. A British journalist, for example, responded to the pamphlet by stating, "The press accounts you send me do indeed move me to protest against the conditions which make such occurrences possible. These cases seem when one reads them to be of peculiar brutality and to one who like myself, has a particular fondness for the American people, almost incredible." Another British editor replied, "I have received copies of the newspaper reports of the terrible lynching affair. It has filled me with a feeling of disgust, which I would fain hope is felt by the vast majority of the white population in the United States."[68]

Most interestingly, the NAACP forwarded copies of "An American Lynching" to Japanese periodicals, and to the organization's delight, the Tokyo-based *Asian Review* wrote a harsh denunciation of the Henry Lowery lynching and the American hypocrisy it revealed. In unequivocal terms, the *Asian Review* declared,

> Americans claim to be the champions of justice and humanity . . . yet they do not hesitate to trample upon these very principles and perpetuate the foulest deed ever conceived. It is an indelible stain . . . on the name of America that in the enlightened age such crimes should take place publicly and the offenders go unpunished.[69]

The *Asian Review*'s commentary was a public relations victory for the NAACP. Unlike the case of the UK, which had a historic relationship with the United States and where Ida B. Wells had undertaken antilynching speaking tours in the 1890s, there was no equivalent effort made to involve the Japanese public prior

[68] Ibid. For a more detailed analysis of British perceptions and responses to American lynching, see Sarah L. Silkey, "British Public Debates and the 'Americanization' of Lynching," in *Swift to Wrath: Lynching in Global Historical* Perspective, eds. Christopher Waldrep and William Carrigan (Charlottesville: University of Virginia Press, 2013).

[69] Zangrando, Papers of the NAACP, reel 2, frames 0791–0845. See also, "Japan Condemns American Lynchings," *Philadelphia Tribune*, July 16, 1921. For a detailed and nuanced analysis of the Japanese government's and Japanese media's stance on the lynching of African Americans, see Marc Gallicchio, *The African American Encounter with Japan and China: Black Internationalism in Asia, 1895–1945* (Chapel Hill: University of North Carolina Press, 2000), and Fumiko Sakashita, "Lynching across the Pacific: Japanese Views and African American Responses in the Wartime Anti-Lynching Campaign," in *Swift to Wrath: Lynching in Global Historical Perspective*, eds. Waldrep and Carrigan.

to the "An American Lynching" pamphlet. The *Asian Review*'s uncompromising stance on the issue of lynching likely suggested to the NAACP that their efforts to publicize lynching were beginning to reap enormous political fruit.

Americans and international newspapers' positive reception of "An American Lynching" suggested that the NAACP's victimization narrative of the lynched black body had inspired the shock and revulsion that the organization had hoped for. Unlike black newspaper coverage that portrayed Lowery's manly defiance of the lynch mob, the NAACP's "An American Lynching" emphasized the graphic details of Lowery burning at the stake in order to convey how black lynch victims were dehumanized by the white lynch mob violence. Furthermore, the pamphlet framed Lowery as a perfect victim of white lynch mob violence by presenting news reports that suggested how both Lowery and police authorities were helpless to prevent the lynching. In all these ways, "An American Lynching" sought to position white audiences to embrace Henry Lowery – and by extension other black lynch victims – as deserving of pity and protection from white lynch mob violence. However, in foregrounding the fact that "An American Lynching" reprinted white newspaper reports of the Henry Lowery lynching without commentary, the organization was calculating that black suffering would become intelligible and meaningful to white audiences only if it were described and verified by whites. In the months following the Henry Lowery lynching and the "An American Lynching" publicity campaign, the NAACP hoped that its efforts to transform the hearts and minds of white Americans through a black victimization narrative of the lynched black body would bear political fruit in the guise of a federal antilynching bill.

CONCLUSION

Exactly one year to the day from when Henry Lowery was lynched in Nodena, Arkansas, the United States House of Representatives passed the nation's first antilynching bill. Although the date of the legislation was purely coincidental, it is a herald of the ways in which Henry Lowery's case helped frame for Congress and the American public the necessity for stringent antilynching enforcement.[70]

[70] See "38 Lynched while Congress Debates Anti-Lynching Bill," *Baltimore Afro-American*, December 21, 1921, for an additional example as to how the NAACP used Henry Lowery's lynching to pressure the House of Representatives to pass a federal antilynching bill.

The 1922 Dyer Anti-Lynching Bill made lynching a federal crime, which consequently empowered the federal government to prosecute both lynchers and state authorities who idly stood by and watched them occur. Between Lowery's lynching in January 1921 and the passage of the House antilynching bill in January 1922, the NAACP stepped up its lobbying efforts within Congress by selectively publicizing the most sensational lynchings.[71] Once the bill had passed in the House, black newspapers carried editorials and articles criticizing Congress for their snail-like response. Using a strategy much like that of the NAACP's "An American Lynching" campaign, black newspapers suggested that black Americans would continue being lynched unless Congress acted.[72]

Despite the fact that the Dyer bill was ultimately sidelined in the Senate, the NAACP realized that its most important leverage among stalwart congressmen was its ability to shape public opinion on the issue of lynching and more specifically white public opinion concerning the lynched black body. In the "An American Lynching" campaign, the NAACP's fundamental objective had been to help whites reimagine the lynched black body beyond the narrow strictures of the black beast rapist discourse, because in white popular opinion (even among whites who abhorred lynching), the black beast rapist and the lynched black body seemingly went hand in hand. In order to reframe the lynched black body in a way that elicited white sympathy rather than derision, the NAACP's "An American Lynching" campaign stressed how seemingly all-powerful white mobs lynched helpless black Americans. Therefore, in the place of the black beast rapist narrative, the NAACP offered a victimization narrative of the lynched black body that framed it as primarily an object of white sympathy rather than as a historical agent. In other words, the victimization narrative of the lynched black body portrayed black lynch victims, and by extension all blacks, as perfect victims of white mob violence. However, the "An American Lynching" publicity campaign spawned by the Lowery case was not the first appearance of the victimization narrative, nor would it be the last. In 1910, Chicago-based black activists, led by Ida B. Wells,

[71] See Raiford, *Imprisoned in a Luminous Glare*, 29–33.

[72] "While Congress Debates the Anti-Lynching Bill," *Baltimore Afro-American*, February 10, 1922; "Burned at the Stake: While the Senate Debates," *Baltimore Afro-American*, May 26, 1922.

successfully employed the specter of the lynched black body in order to win a court injunction preventing Steve Green's return to Arkansas. Given that Columbia University professor Joel Spingarn's involvement in the Green case led him to join the NAACP and ultimately became one of the organization's most important financial backers for its antilynching activism and otherwise, it is safe to assume that Steve Green's case made an indelible – though largely unacknowledged – contribution to the antilynching movement.

To be sure, the NAACP's embrace and perpetuation of the victimization narrative of the lynched black body was politically expedient. Since the NAACP calculated that for whites an empowered black body could only be one that threatened white interests, a dehumanized and disempowered black body would both assuage white fears as well as propel whites toward a more sympathetic view of black lynch victims. But although the victimization narrative was politically expedient, it could not be the basis for articulating a usable past for African Americans grappling with the cultural and psychological trauma that lynching wrought. For dealing with this aspect of lynching, black Americans turned to black writers and themselves to fashion consoling narratives of the lynched black body.

3

If We Must Die

Black-authored victimization narratives of the lynched black body emphasized how white mobs lynched black Americans with impunity and seized upon the various ways in which white-on-black lynch mob violence dehumanized powerless blacks. In the context of the antilynching movement, victimization narratives aimed to prevent lynchings in the making as well as create national and international political support for federal antilynching legislation. Although victimization narratives were politically expedient, they had limited use for creating a sense of empowerment among black Americans attempting to cope with white lynch mob violence. Consoling narratives of the lynched black body filled this void. In contrast with victimization narratives, which stressed what *white lynchers did* to black lynch victims, consoling narratives emphasized what *black lynch victims did* in response to white lynch mob violence. In general, consoling narratives focused on how black lynch victims violently defended themselves against white lynch mob actions and often detailed how black lynch victims killed several lynchers before they were lynched. To be sure, consoling narratives of the lynched black body were not triumphant narratives in which blacks escaped lynching because they fought back. To the contrary, literary consoling narratives of the lynched black body were invariably those in which black lynch victims were brutally murdered by white lynch mobs. However, in highlighting how black characters violently fought back despite the inevitability of lynching, consoling narratives helped black Americans conceive of white-on-black lynchings as expressions of black heroism. Consoling narratives illustrated the ways in which black Americans had conquered the terror, through violent resistance, that white-on-black lynchings sought to inspire. By presenting the transcending of the fear of a violent death at the hands of white lynchers, consoling narratives asserted that blacks were victims of lynching but not necessarily perfect victims of white lynch mob violence. In doing so, the narratives sought to transform white-on-black lynchings from a symbol of black death to a symbol of black empowerment.

In order to illustrate the above-mentioned themes, I explicate three representative examples of consoling narratives of the lynched black body. The chapter's opening section analyzes Ida B. Wells's "Mob Rule in New Orleans." It explains how the book initiated the tradition of consoling narratives of the lynched black body. The second section examines novelist Sutton Griggs's *The Hindered Hand: Or the Reign of the Repressionist*, and the third and final section reviews Richard Wright's collection of novellas in *Uncle Tom's Children*. Through a careful analysis of these examples, I will argue that the tradition of consoling narratives of the lynched black body reframed black lynch victims as powerful symbols of resistance and black empowerment.

MOB RULE IN NEW ORLEANS

Jamaican-born poet Claude McKay's "If We Must Die" (1921) is one of best-known protest poems of the early twentieth century. It is also a consoling narrative of the lynched black body. For instance, McKay's militant poem urged black Americans to violently resist white terrorism. McKay wrote,

> If we must die, let it not be like hogs
> Hunted and penned in an inglorious spot
> . . . .
> If we must die, O let us nobly die,
> So that our precious blood may not be shed
> In vain; then even the monsters we defy
> Shall be constrained to honor us though dead!
> . . . .
> Though far outnumbered let us show us brave,
> And for their thousand blows deal one deathblow!
> . . . .

> Like men we'll face the murderous, cowardly pack,
> Pressed to the wall, dying, but fighting back![1]

On one level, "If We Must Die" was meant to challenge white supremacist constructions of African American men as brutes and cowards; however, McKay's primary purpose was to assert that the lynching spectacle presented African American men with a choice of dying honorably. It is a forgone conclusion that death is inevitable and that resistance will not save the lynched black body, but McKay asserted that black lynch victims must fight back anyway. In fact, McKay suggested that lynched black bodies accrued honor because they violently fought back knowing that their resistance was futile and would likely further embolden white lynchers to exact more torture. For McKay, dying a noble death hinged upon choosing that it "not to be like hogs, hunted and penned in an inglorious spot," but rather offering resistance to white lynchers that would assert the race's manhood through this courageous choice. Therefore, in choosing to fight back, McKay suggested that African American lynch victims would transform lynching narratives from stories of black brutalization to stories of black masculine courage.

In his poem, Claude McKay suggested that suffering a violent death does not necessarily victimize; rather, how one responds to violence determines whether one was victimized or not. McKay was not the first black writer to make this case. Approximately twenty years earlier, Ida B. Wells forcefully articulated this position in the aftermath of the lynching of Robert Charles in New Orleans, Louisiana. On July 23, 1900, Robert Charles and Leonard Pierce were involved in an altercation with New Orleans police that led to them fatally shooting and killing two officers. After a four-day manhunt for Robert Charles, police set ablaze the New Orleans home in which Charles had barricaded himself. In his attempt to flee the burning house, he was shot and subdued. Subsequently, Charles's body was repeatedly shot and beaten by a white mob that had gathered to lynch him.[2] Local and national white newspaper reports portrayed Robert Charles as a negro desperado who resisted arrest and wantonly killed two white officers. For instance, the *Chicago Tribune* editorialized, "There will be no

[1] For the full text of Claude McKay's "If We Must Die," see Anne Rice, ed., *Witnessing Lynching: American Writers Respond* (New Brunswick: Rutgers University Press, 2003), 190.

[2] For a detailed reconstruction of the lynching of Robert Charles, see William Ivy Hair's *Carnival of Fury: Robert Charles and the New Orleans Race Riot of 1900* (Baton Rouge: Louisiana State University Press, 2008).

sympathy expressed for Robert Charles.... He was a worthless negro, and more than that, a desperate criminal." Other white newspapers echoed the *Tribune*'s sentiments.[3]

Within months of the lynching, Wells published a pamphlet entitled "Mob Rule in New Orleans." It provided a searing counternarrative that refuted white newspaper depictions of Charles as a desperado and instead argued that he was a courageous, hardworking individual who selflessly defended his life against an unwarranted police arrest and mob violence.[4] The bulk of Wells's counternarrative carefully showed how the white press distorted the actions that led to the melee between the New Orleans police and Robert Charles as well as his motivations for shooting the police officers and fleeing arrest. Wells stated,

> The policemen, however, secure in the firm belief that they could do anything to a Negro that they wished, approached the two men [Robert Charles and Leonard Pierce], and in less than three minutes from the time they accosted them attempted to put both colored men under arrest. Charles was made victim of a savage attack by Officer Mora, who used a billet and then drew a gun and tried to kill Charles. Charles drew his gun nearly as quickly as the policeman, and began a duel in the street, in which both participants were shot. The police got the worst of the duel, and fell helpless to the sidewalk. Charles made his escape.[5]

Wells goes on to assert,

> In any law-abiding community Charles would have been justified in delivering himself up immediately to the properly constituted authorities and asking a trial by a jury of his peers. He could have been certain that in resisting an unwarranted arrest he had a right to defend his life, even to the point of taking one in that defense, but Charles knew that his arrest in New Orleans, even for defending his life, meant nothing short of a long term in the penitentiary, and still more probable death by lynching at the hands of a cowardly mob.[6]

[3] "New Orleans Race Riot," *Chicago Daily Tribune*, July 29, 1900; "Shot at His Pursuers," *Washington Post*, July 28, 1900; "Murderer Charles Captured," *New York Times*, July 27, 1900.

[4] For an alternative reading of Wells's "Mob Rule in New Orleans" that emphasizes how the pamphlet employed parody to undermine the cultural logic of white newspaper portrayals of Robert Charles, see Jacqueline Goldsby, *A Spectacular Secret: Lynching in American Life and Literature* (Chicago: University of Chicago Press, 2006), 94–100.

[5] Ida B. Wells-Barnett and Patricia Hill Collins, *On Lynchings* (Amherst: Humanity Books, 2002), 155.

[6] Ibid., 156.

Not only did Wells provide a rationalization for Robert Charles's refusal to submit to arrest and his subsequent flight, but she also endeavored to counter racist representations of Charles as a ruthless lawbreaker. In the white supremacist imagination, black desperadoes were portrayed as irrationally violent men who had little regard for their own lives or the lives of others; therefore, spectacular violence was necessary to suppress them.[7] In order to deflect white newspaper portrayals of Charles as a criminal, Wells investigated Charles's background and found several white character witnesses to attest that he was a peaceful and law-abiding individual.[8] Moreover, Wells highlighted Charles's courage and manliness by suggesting that despite superior numbers and better-armed whites, Charles bravely refused to submit to arrest even as he was cornered by a lynch mob. Wells marveled at the fact that as Charles shot at mob participants, he forced them to flee for cover in a cowardly manner. According to Wells, Robert Charles shot twenty-four white men and killed seven of them (including four policemen) during the weeklong standoff.[9] In this way, Wells implied that white newspapers' celebration of mob participants as courageous was nothing more than a pretense. For example,

> Betrayed into the hands of the police, Charles, who had already sent two of his would-be murders to their death, made a last stand in a small building, 1210 Saratoga Street, and, still defying his pursuers, fought a mob of twenty thousand people, single-handed and alone, killing three more men, mortally wounding two more and seriously wounding nine others. Unable to get him in his stronghold, the besiegers set fire to his house of refuge. While the building was burning Charles was shooting, and every crack of his death-dealing rifle added another victim to the price which he had placed upon his own life. Finally, when fire and smoke became too much for flesh and blood to stand, the long sought for fugitive appeared in the door, rifle in hand, to charge the countless guns that were drawn upon him. With a courage which was indescribable, he raised his guns to fire again, but this time it failed, for a hundred shots riddled his body, and he fell dead face fronting to the mob.[10]

[7] See George Fredrickson, *The Black Image in the White Mind: The Debate on Afro-American Character and Destiny, 1817–1914* (New York: Harper and Row, 1971), 278–279, and Sandra Gunning's *Race, Rape, and Lynching*, chapter 1.

[8] Wells and Collins, *On Lynchings*, 195–197.

[9] Hair, *Carnival of Fury*, 171.

[10] Wells and Collins, *On Lynchings*, 170–171.

Wells concluded, "The white people of this country may charge that he was a desperado, but to the people of his own race Robert Charles will always be regarded as the hero of New Orleans."[11] Wells's extensive praise of Robert Charles's actions and her depiction of him as a hero suggest that she believed that he provided a militant model for other African American men to follow. Following her interpretation of the incident, New Orleans blacks – and ultimately black Southerners – would sing "the Robert Charles song" at all-black gathering as a means of paying homage to a black man who had stood up valiantly to white intransigence.[12]

The depiction of the lynched black body as masculine heroism shared some affinities with the much older "bad nigger" legend in black folklore and fiction. The classic bad nigger archetype was male, callously violent, a bully and braggart, fearless in the face of danger, and above all one that flouted white authority. He might mock or even kill whites depending upon what the situation called for or what his mood dictated. The classic bad nigger lived to be "ba-ad," and "bad-ness" was his only currency.[13] This model represents a machismo ideal in which true manhood is rooted in both the exaggerated embrace of masculine virtues (such a strength and courage) and the flouting of any and all normative conventions of manhood that might subdue those qualities. In part, Robert Charles's notoriety among blacks may have sprung from the fact that he was a peaceful and law-abiding citizen but became a bad nigger when confronted with wanton white violence. Yet although Ida B. Wells's Robert Charles (and, as we shall see later, Sutton Griggs's Gus and Richard Wright's Silas) exhibited aspects of the bad nigger persona, he was categorically different from the classic bad nigger in that he employed violence as primarily a cathartic expression of his humanity rather than simply as a means of showing his contempt for white deference and social normativity or to exhibit badness for badness' sake.

In addition to debunking racist representations of Robert Charles and African American men more generally, Wells's "Mob Rule in

[11] Ibid., 197.

[12] Hair, *Carnival of Fury*, 178.

[13] Jerry H. Bryant, *Born in a Mighty Bad Land: The Violent Man in African American Folklore and Fiction* (Bloomington: Indiana University Press, 2003), 1–7 and 10–12. See also John Roberts, *From Trickster to Badman: The Black Folk Hero in Slavery and Freedom* (Philadelphia: University of Pennsylvania Press, 1989).

New Orleans" is historically significant because it marked an apparent shift in Wells's understanding of white supremacy. In Wells's initial speeches and writings during the 1890s, she assumed that white Americans were an inherently moral and upright race and that their tacit acceptance of lynching was due to having the wrong ideas about black people. Through her antilynching activism (of which her pamphlets were a cornerstone), Wells believed that if she could reveal the truth about lynching to whites, consequently whites would cease to lynch black people. Wells's strident tone throughout "Mob Rule" suggests that she no longer believed that remedying white ignorance would necessarily have a salutary effect on white mob lynching; thus, African Americans had to rely on themselves and their institutions to prevent mob violence.

Wells's overt pessimism concerning the possibility of reforming white attitudes signaled a changing cultural politics of the lynched black body. Specifically, Wells was the first antilynching activist-writer to catalog in a lengthy piece of writing how an actual lynch victim violently fought back against white lynch mob violence – with the intention of reframing the lynched black body as a symbol of heroic black masculinity. To be sure, predecessors to Wells (such as John Edward Bruce, John Mitchell Jr., and T. Thomas Fortune, to name a few) had at one time or another advocated armed resistance as a necessary response to racial violence.[14] Perhaps most

[14] For an excellent discussion of African American journalists' views on armed self-defense and its relationship to black manhood at the turn of the twentieth century, see Kidada E. Williams, *They Left Great Marks on Me*, 117–133. For a comprehensive overview of black leaders' perspectives on lynching prior to Ida B. Wells, see Herbert Shapiro, *White Violence and the Black Response: From Reconstruction to Montgomery* (Amherst: University of Massachusetts Press, 1988), especially chapter 2. For detailed biographical treatments of John Mitchell Jr., John Edward Bruce, and T. Thomas Fortune, see the following titles: Ann Field Alexander, *Race Man: The Rise and Fall of the "Fighting Editor," John Mitchell Jr.* (Charlottesville: University of Virginia Press, 2002), especially chapters 4 and 5; Peter Gilbert, *The Selected Writings of John Edward Bruce: Militant Black Journalist* (New York: Arno Press/New York Times, 1971), especially 29–32; William Seraile, *Bruce Grit: Black Nationalist Writings of John Edward Bruce* (Knoxville: University of Tennessee Press, 2003); Ralph L. Crowder, *John Edward Bruce: Politician, Journalist, and Self-Trained Historian of the African Diaspora* (New York: New York University Press, 2004); Shawn Leigh Alexander, ed., *T. Thomas Fortune, The Afro-American Agitator: A Collection of Writings, 1880–1928* (Gainesville: University Press of Florida, 2008), especially chapters 13 and 14; Emma Lou Thornborough, *T. Thomas Fortune: Militant Journalist*

emphatically, in a fiery 1889 speech, journalist John Edward Bruce proclaimed, "The man who will not fight for the protection of his wife and children is a coward and deserves to be ill treated. The man who takes his life in his hand and stands up for what he knows to be right will always command the respect of his enemy." Bruce emphasized this point by declaring,

> If they burn your houses, burn theirs. If they kill your wives and children, kill theirs. Pursue them relentlessly. Meet force with force, everywhere it is offered. If they demand blood, exchange with them until they are satiated. By a vigorous adherence to this course, the shedding of human blood by white men will soon become a thing of the past.[15]

For Bruce and other black leaders who advocated armed resistance, black armed resistance to white lynch mob violence was the surest way to curb it, whereas black docility was the surest way to encourage it. In addition, Bruce implied that black men who employed armed resistance in response to racial violence asserted the race's manhood. And Wells certainly echoed these sentiments in her earlier antilynching pamphlets.[16] However, in "Mob Rule," Wells broke new ground by articulating how armed resistance might be employed to memorialize the lynched black body as an exemplar of heroic manhood. In doing so, Wells initiated the genre of consoling narratives of the lynched black body.[17]

In general, "Mob Rule in New Orleans" consoled African American audiences by reframing the lynched black body as a historical agent. Wells accomplished this by portraying Robert Charles as displaying uncommon manly courage and prowess (in contrast with the cowardly mob) by killing numerous members of the frenzied crowd that encircled him. Rather than commit suicide or attempt to flee by some other means, Wells proclaimed that Robert Charles had died a manly and noble death by facing the mob head on and fighting to his last breath. In so doing, Wells emphasized that Robert Charles's (and by extension other lynch

(Chicago: University of Chicago Press, 1972); and Waldrep, *African Americans Confront Lynching*, especially chapter 2.

[15] Shapiro, *White Violence and the Black Response*, 42.

[16] Wells and Collins, *On Lynchings*, 50.

[17] See Rebecca Hill, *Men, Mobs, and the Law: Anti-Lynching and Labor Defense in U.S. Radical History* (Durham: Duke University Press, 2009), 133. Rebecca Hill asserts that Wells's framing of black lynch victims as exhibiting manly heroism drew on a much earlier abolitionists' tradition.

victims') citizenship rights and manhood could not be stripped away through violently murdering them.

"Mob Rule in New Orleans" concludes with Wells referring to Robert Charles as the "hero of New Orleans." For Wells, reframing Robert Charles as an exemplar of heroic manhood was about the power of claiming dignity and hope through the most potent symbol of white supremacy and black degradation. If black people could retain a sense of dignity and hope in face of the lynched black body, then black humanity was incontrovertible. If black humanity was incontrovertible, then the lynched black body could be envisioned as a powerful symbol of black transcendence. Wells's narrative of the Robert Charles lynching underscores the idea that lynched blacks were not powerless, perfect victims easily victimized by white mobs, but rather black lynch victims and black people in general could claim a sense of power and even superiority in defeat. In this way, Wells's "Mob Rule" pamphlet transformed white-on-black lynchings from a symbol of black death to a symbol of black empowerment.

"Mob Rule in New Orleans" pioneered a new approach to challenging white supremacist narratives of the lynched black body with a basic framework that black writers, and particularly black fiction writers, would later appropriate and transform. In the early twentieth century, a cadre of black writers recognized that the lynched black body as a dehumanized subject would continue to cast a shadow over black subjectivity as long as they did not find ways to reimagine it. For these writers, dealing with the cultural residue of the lynched black body involved more than simply denouncing lynching and its incompatibility with American ideals. More fundamentally, black subjectivity had to be reframed and redeployed in light of the lynched black body. In varying degrees, early twentieth-century black writers constructed consoling narratives of the lynched black body in their novels, short stories, and poems in an effort to reimagine the lynched black body as something more than a symbol of powerlessness and dehumanization.[18] In what follows, I will discuss how novelists

[18] See, K. Mitchell, *Living with Lynching*, particularly chapters 1 and 5. In addition to black novelists' and poets' construction of consoling narratives of the lynched black body, Koritha Mitchell has compellingly made the case that black-authored lynching plays that were communally staged provided resources that helped African Americans survive the lynching era believing in their right to full citizenship. The key difference in black-authored lynching plays and black-authored

Sutton Griggs and Richard Wright appropriated and redeployed the idea of consoling narratives of the lynched black body that was initiated by Ida B. Wells.

HINDERED HANDS

Sutton Griggs's *The Hindered Hand: Or the Reign of the Repressionist* (1905) deserves careful consideration, because he was the first major black novelist to feature lynching in his writings as well as the first to pen a literary response to Thomas Dixon's *The Leopard's Spots* (1902), which unapologetically rationalizes the lynching of black Americans. Griggs's *The Hindered Hand* carefully refutes *The Leopard's Spots*' antiblack rationales for lynching and explores whether black Americans should employ violent resistance or peaceful approaches to upending white mob violence. Griggs was devoted to peaceful approaches to resolving the race problem, and therefore he does not depict in the novel black violent resistance in response to white lynch mob violence. Nonetheless, *The Hindered Hand* fits squarely within the tradition of consoling narratives of the lynched black body because Griggs emphasizes black agency in response to white mob violence.

Sutton Elbert Griggs was born in Chatfield, Texas, on June 19, 1872. His father, Allen R. Griggs, was a Baptist preacher in Texas. Griggs attended public school in Dallas before graduating from Bishop College in 1890. From there, Griggs attended Richmond Theological Seminary and accepted a pastorate at the First Baptist Church in Berkley, Virginia, upon graduation. In 1895, he moved to Nashville to accept the pastorate at the First Baptist Church there.[19] Griggs's militant phase occurred between 1895 and 1908 when he was a pastor in Nashville. Due in part to his writing and oratory, he was considered by many to be an outspoken racial leader. For instance, literary historian Arlene Elder noted: "With a brilliant mind and a ready pen, Doctor Griggs went to the fray in such

fiction is that black-authored fiction is replete with dramatic reenactments of white-on-black lynching, whereas lynching plays displaced the lynching spectacle and, rather, dramatized how black families (particularly women) coped with the aftermath of lynching. In doing so, Mitchell asserts that lynching plays affirmed the value of black personhood and thereby made it possible to live with lynching.

[19] Arlene A. Elder, *The "Hindered Hand": Cultural Implications of Early African-American Fiction* (Westport: Greenwood Press, 1978), 70.

a militant fashion that he was almost termed a radical on racial matters. He was acclaimed as a champion in all sections and his appearances before the sessions of other religious groups were occasions of wild demonstrations of enthusiastic approval."[20]

During this period, Griggs's major publications included *Imperium in Imperio* (1899), *Overshadowed* (1901), *Unfettered* (1902), *The Hindered Hand* (1905), and *Pointing the Way* (1908). Collectively, his literary canon sought to provide a blueprint for black political action and narrate the complexities of black identity as well as describe both the internal and external conditions that threatened black society in the late nineteenth and early twentieth centuries. Griggs's emphasis on these themes emerged in response to racial segregation and white violence against blacks. Accordingly, he proposed that blacks ought to strive for psychological, social, and economic independence. Yet his calls for black self-determination belied his belief that racial progress depended upon "conservative pragmatism" and particularly political cooperation between conservative black and white leaders.[21]

W. E. B. Du Bois and other black contemporaries noted that Griggs's body of work appealed primarily to the black masses. Although his upbringing was one more akin to that of the black middle class, his position as a pastor allowed him to develop an intimate knowledge of black working-class life and culture. In addition, his relationship to the working class was strengthened through his reliance on the educated black working class to purchase his novels and essays. For instance, Griggs was known to sell his materials door to door, on black college campuses, and at black places of employment during lunch hours. Although he depended upon the black working class to purchase his books, however, he also believed that literature should serve the black working class. In particular, he believed that it could provide a basis for racial unity as well as inspire a new generation of educated and principled black leaders.[22]

20 Ibid., 70–71.

21 Ibid., 69–70. For a fuller explanation and analysis of how Griggs deployed "conservative pragmatism" throughout his novels, see Finnie D. Coleman, *Sutton E. Griggs and the Struggle against White Supremacy* (Knoxville: University of Tennessee Press, 2007), viii and especially chapter 3.

22 Wilson J. Moses, "Literary Garveyism: The Novels of Reverend Sutton E. Griggs," *Pylon* 40 (1979): 204–205, 213; Coleman, *Sutton E. Griggs*, 17, 21.

In 1905, Griggs published *The Hindered Hand* at the request of the National Baptist Convention, which believed that Griggs was best suited to pen a literary response to Thomas Dixon's popular romance *The Leopard's Spots*.[23] Published in 1902, *The Leopard's Spots* appeared as Southern legislatures chipped away at black voting rights at the turn of the twentieth century. During this period, Dixon and other prominent Southern writers led a literary movement to justify disenfranchisement, and *The Leopard's Spots* epitomizes turn-of-the-century Negrophobia. Throughout the novel, he portrays African Americans as thieves, parasites, and even "A Thousand-Legged Beast."[24] The novel's main contention is that black people were unfit for citizenship because they were degenerating back to their savage African heritage. In making this argument, Dixon developed a scathing attack on the black church and the black family. He dismissed black education as a means of uplifting individuals and instead asserted that its primary concern was for black men to achieve interracial marriage with white women. Moreover, he belittled black veterans returning from the Spanish American War and justified spectacle lynching as a necessary social control mechanism.[25]

Throughout *The Hindered Hand*, Griggs refutes each of Dixon's racist depictions of black life. In doing so, he explores three primary approaches to uprooting the racial caste system: passing as white, armed resistance, and political agitation. With regard to passing, the plot revolves around the mixed race Seabright family, which, interestingly, migrates to the South in order to escape racial prejudice in the North. As a mixed-race family that looks white in appearance, the Seabrights easily establish themselves within the Southern white elite. The matriarch, Mrs. Seabright, plans to use the family's position within the white elite to curtail race prejudice. She cultivates a marriage between Eunice, her daughter, and

[23] Thomas Dixon Jr., *The Leopard's Spots, a Romance of the White Man's Burden, 1865–1900* (New York: Doubleday, 1902). For a broader analysis of African Americans' response to Thomas Dixon's literary work, see John David Smith, "'My Books Are Hard Reading for a Negro': Tom Dixon and His African American Critics, 1905–1939," in *Thomas Dixon Jr. and the Birth of Modern America*, eds. Michele K. Gillespie and Randall L. Hall (Baton Rouge: Louisiana State University, 2006).

[24] Hugh M. Gloster, "Sutton E. Griggs: Novelist of the New Negro," *Pylon* 4 (1943): 335–336.

[25] Geraldine Hord Seay, "The Literature of Jim Crow: Call and Response" (PhD diss., University of Florida, 1996), 111.

a prominent white politician, who will be an unwitting pawn in their plans. However, before the plan can proceed further, Eunice inexplicably flees her husband. The Seabrights' plan subsequently unravels when Eunice's husband finds her, charges her with bigamy, and discovers that she is mixed race. Upon hearing this news, her husband disowns her. Thereafter, Eunice and the Seabright family are forced to endure the indignities of racial prejudice.

The novel's dramatic tension revolves around several lynching scenes and how black characters respond to lynch mob violence.[26] In depicting white lynch mob violence, Griggs challenges the legitimacy of lynching by illustrating how innocent blacks were lynched for unwittingly challenging white supremacy. For example, Henry Crump, a fourteen-year-old boy, is the first of three lynching victims in the novel. As Crump is walking to school, he is harassed by a group of white children. Though Crump momentarily stands his ground, he walks away to avoid trouble. In response, the white children begin to pelt him with stones. In defense, he returns a volley of stones in their direction. Unbeknownst to Henry, a police officer spots him throwing stones at the white children, and he is arrested and jailed. At his trial, the judge fines him $25 but rescinds it after the Crump family immediately pays the fine. Sensing that the Crump family is attempting to upstage him, the judge sentences Henry to hard labor on a prison farm. Henry Crump panics, flees the courtroom, and temporarily escapes but is later surrounded by the police. Although he appears to have surrendered, one of the white spectators who gather to witness the chase shoots and kills him. Whites in attendance murmur, "Shame! Shame! Shame!" when they realize Crump is dead; however, Crump's killer goes unpunished.[27] In the novel's second lynching, Dave Harper is falsely accused of murdering Arlene Daleman, a prominent white woman. Initially, he is captured and jailed, but later a white police officer hands him over to a lynch mob. Subsequently, the mob hangs him from a post and repeatedly fires bullets into his body.[28]

Griggs further undermines the legitimacy of lynching by highlighting its barbarity in the novel's third lynching. In this example, Bud Harper and Foresta Harper flee to Mississippi and

[26] Ibid., 140–154.

[27] Sutton E. Griggs, *The Hindered Hand: Or the Reign of The Repressionist* (Whitefish: Kessinger Publishing, 2007), 53–61.

[28] Ibid., 104–107.

assume new identities when they discover that a lynch mob has intended to lynch Bud but mistakenly lynched his twin brother, Dave Harper, the victim of the book's second lynching. While in Mississippi, the Harpers' presence raises the ire of local whites; consequently, whites hire Sidney Fletcher to kill both Bud and Foresta. In self-defense, Bud shoots and kills Fletcher. Fully realizing that they will be lynched if they remain, the couple again flees but is eventually caught and burned at the stake. Griggs's description of the Harper double lynching is a near-verbatim adaptation of the 1904 Luther Holbert lynching in Doddsville, Mississippi, as originally reported in the *Vicksburg Evening Post*.[29] Griggs writes,

> The mob decided to torture their victims before killing them and began on Foresta first. A man with a pair of scissors stepped up and cut off her hair and threw it into the crowd. There was a great scramble for bits of hair for souvenirs of the occasion. One by one her fingers were cut off and tossed into the crowd to be scrambled for. A man with a cork screw came forward, ripped Foresta's clothing to her waist, bored into her breast with corkscrew and pulled forth the live quivering flesh. Poor Bud her helpless husband closed his eyes and turned away his head to avoid the terrible sight. Men gathered about him and forced his eyelids open so that he could see all.
>
> When it was thought that Foresta had been tortured sufficiently, attention was turned to Bud. His fingers were cut off one by one and corkscrew was bored into his legs and arms. A man with a club struck him over the head, crushing his skull and forcing an eyeball to hang down from the socket by a thread. A rush was made toward Bud and a man who was a little ahead of his competitors snatched the eyeball as a souvenir.[30]

As this passage suggests, Griggs highlights Bud and Foresta Harper's elaborate torture ritual in order to demonstrate how white mobs dehumanized and emasculated the lynched black body. For Griggs and other black writers, torture rituals mattered insofar as they made manifest black vulnerability and white sadism. However, given how Griggs emphasizes Bud Harper closing his eyes to avoid watching his wife's torture and the mob forcing him to watch, it appears that it is not so much about the intense pain that is unleashed upon the lynched black body that is most important, but rather it is the lynched black body succumbing to that pain. Surrendering to pain symbolized that whites effectively gained

[29] T. Harris, *Exorcising Blackness*, 2.
[30] Griggs, *The Hindered Hand*, 133–134.

power over the lynched black body and that black lynched subjects effectively lost control. Thus, Bud Harper is reduced to a powerless witness, and his only possible response is to feel a deep sense of emptiness and shame. Griggs suggests that in the white imagination there was an inverse relationship between black powerlessness and white empowerment: the more the lynched black body was defiled, the more powerful the white lynch mob became. In addition, Bud and Foresta's dismemberment underscores the dehumanization of the lynched black body as their bodies are disaggregated and reconstituted as souvenirs. Interestingly, Griggs suggests that through the dismantling of black bodies, the white supremacist body or white manhood is consolidated. The burning of Bud and Foresta's bodies consummates the victory over deviant black bodies and ensures that their final moments will end in excruciating agony.

Griggs further underscores lynching's barbarity by depicting white children's sadistic appetite for witnessing lynching. Prior to Bud and Foresta Harper's lynching, Melville Brant, a nine-year-old white child, begs his mother to take him to the lynching. Melville's motivation for attending the lynching stems from his belief that Ben Stringer, his white companion, has witnessed lynchings and is therefore held in higher regard among their playmates. In protest, Melville's mother locks him in the attic, but he escapes and joins his friends at the lynching anyway. In the aftermath of the lynching, Melville finds a charred piece of the lynch victim's flesh and triumphantly rejoices, "Ben Stinger ain't got nothing on me now."[31] Furthermore, Griggs contrasts Melville Brant's supposed childhood innocence with his sadistic desire to witness the execution and appropriate lynching souvenirs. In doing so, Griggs employs sentimental notions of childhood to make lynching more monstrous.[32]

[31] Ibid., 135.

[32] Clayton Allen Cerny, "Reconstructing Freedom: Romance and Race in American Culture, 1877–1915" (PhD diss., Northwestern University, 1996), 185. Other black writers also highlighted the ways in which the commodification of the black body indoctrinated white youth into white supremacist culture. For example, Bertha Johnson's poem "I Met a Blue-Eyed Girl" depicts the lynched black body as an intimate and valued possession of a five-year-old white girl who carries inside a locket the tooth of a lynched black male; see Rice, *Witnessing Lynching*, 121. Also, Anne Spencer's classic poem "White Things" mentions a white child who claims the skull of a lynched black male as his prize; see, ibid., 235. In addition, for an in-depth study of white Southern youth socialization and lynching, see Kristina DuRocher, *Raising Racists: The Socialization of White Children in the Jim Crow South* (Lexington: University Press of Kentucky, 2011).

Dixon's *The Leopard's Spots* portrays lynching as a necessary response to black retrogression and criminality, and Griggs counters these assertions by depicting black lynch victims as peaceful and law-abiding citizens. In addition, Griggs suggests that lynching is less about black criminality and more about imposing a racial caste system. For instance, in the aftermath of the Harper double lynching, a white spectator admits,

> You want to know how we square the burning of a woman with the statement that we lynch for one crime in the South, heh? That's all rot about one crime. We lynch niggers down here for anything. We lynch them for being sassy and sometimes lynch them on general principles. The truth of the matter is the real "one crime" that paves the way for a lynching whenever we have the notion, is the crime of being black.[33]

In this passage, Griggs utilizes the white spectator's quip to highlight the hypocrisy of white lynch mob violence. Griggs's white spectator willingly acknowledges and embraces the contradiction between the professed reason whites lynched blacks (the rape of white women) and the actual reason whites lynched blacks (being black in a white supremacist society). For Griggs, the lynching of black people did not hinge upon whether they were guilty of a crime or even whether there was an allegation of criminal activity. Lynch mobs, and by extension white Southerners, lynched blacks because of antiblack racial prejudice. Therefore, Griggs draws attention to the contradiction between white rhetoric and practice in order to underscore the depravity of white lynch mobs and the irrationality of lynching.

Following the lynching of the Harpers, those responsible for lynching Bud and Foresta are placed on trial. The identities of those who participated in the lynching are well known, and it is up to an all-white jury to decide their fate. During the trial, a white lawyer makes an impassioned plea to the jury to look beyond their racial prejudice and thereby convict the lynchers. Although the jury unsurprisingly renders a not-guilty verdict, the lawyer's appeal seems to represent Griggs's fundamental hope that American institutions will one day dispense justice impartially.[34]

[33] Griggs, *The Hindered Hand*, 136.

[34] T. Harris, *Exorcising Blackness*, 80; Although the ideas of the author may or may not be represented by the narrator or characters found within literary narratives, it seems that there is less a distinction between Griggs's narrators/characters and his political beliefs. According to Finnie Coleman, "An author's success depends

Griggs's uses the Bud and Foresta Harper lynching to explore how blacks ought to respond to white lynch mob violence. In *The Hindered Hand*, two black leaders hold opposing views within early twentieth-century black political thought: black militancy and black conservatism.[35] Black militancy is represented by Earl Bluefield, who is mixed race and embraces radical politics. He admires Native Americans, because "The dead Indian refusing to be enslaved was a richer heritage to the world than the yielding and thriving Negro."[36] Ensal Ellwood is a pastor of unmixed African ancestry and signifies black conservatism. Ensal believes that if race relations are to be improved, the conservative factions of the black and white races will have to band together and provide a solution to the race problem.

After the Harper double lynching, Earl and Ensal meet to construct a response. Earl proposes emigration but later dismisses the idea because whites would not tolerate a general exodus from the South. He also proposes a general uprising but later abandons that as well because whites have superior resources. However, Earl ultimately recommends capturing the state capitol and a U.S. federal building as a means of forcing the race question into the national conscience. Earl reflects,

> In Almaville here, I have picked a band of five hundred men who are not afraid to die. To-night [*sic*] we shall creep upon yonder hill and take charge of the state capitol. When the city awakes tomorrow morning it will find itself at our mercy. We also have a force of men which will take charge of the United States government building. This will serve to make it a national question.
>
> When called upon to surrender, we shall issue a proclamation setting forth our grievances as a race and demanding that they be righted. Of course, what we shall call for cannot be done at once, and our surrender will be called for. We shall not surrender. Each one of us has solemnly sworn not to come out of the affair alive, even if we have to commit suicide. Our act

heavily upon the creation of characters whom the reader is able to respond to and a narrator whom the reader feels is reliable and trustworthy. Occasionally, Griggs creates successful characters, but his narrators are not always reliable. In fact, there are far too many moments in his fiction where the authorial mask slips and Griggs appears to be serving as author and narrator. In literary circles, it is generally considered poor form to conflate the narrator's voice with that of the author. In Griggs's work, such conflation is almost inevitable and unavoidable." Coleman, *Sutton E. Griggs*, 39.

[35] Elder, *The "Hindered Hand,"* 101.

[36] Griggs, *The Hindered Hand*, 49.

will open the eyes of the American people to the gravity of this question and they will act. Once in motion I am not afraid of what they will do. I am not fearful of America awake, but America asleep.[37]

Ensal wholly rejects Earl's plan, because he believes it would certainly invite a general slaughter of innocent black people. Ensal believes that whites are inherently morally upright and that they simply need to be awakened to the plight of blacks. However, in contrast with Earl, Ensal proposes to distribute a pamphlet to every white person to educate them about the race problem, to convince them that black equality is the best course of action. Although swayed by Ensal's impassioned speech, Earl contends that a moral appeal has to be supplemented with brute force, and thus he reaffirms his commitment to capturing government institutions.

Later in the novel, Ensal intercedes to stop the planned takeover of the government buildings. Consequently, a physical struggle ensues, culminating in Ensal accidentally shooting Earl in the side. With Earl subdued, Ensal successfully foils the plot but subsequently decides to immigrate to Africa. Despite Griggs's opposition to armed resistance (as suggested by the foiled plot), Ensal physically assaults Earl to prevent the assault on the state capitol. This is an ironic twist that Griggs did not explore further, and it might suggest his conflicted feelings toward violence as a strategy for black liberation. Even though Ensal thwarts Earl's plot to violently take control of a state building, Griggs indicates Earl's determination by demonstrating that Ensal (who preferred peaceable means to solve problems) had to violently confront and subdue Earl in order to squelch the plot. In doing so, Griggs implies Earl's courage and heroism, particularly given that Earl admits to Ensal that he and his coconspirators have pledged not to come out of the affair alive.

Gus Martin represents a third view. Unlike Ensal, Gus discounts Christianity because it "unmanned" the race. Furthermore, unlike Earl, he despises the idea of patriotism, despite the fact that he served bravely during the Spanish-American War. And contrary to both Earl and Ensal, he asserts that group action (whether conservative or radical) is doomed to failure, and therefore he favors individual and targeted acts of defiance.[38] For example, Gus murders a black man who was passing as white, because he saw the other man kiss a black woman. Gus proceeds to barricade himself within an armory and

[37] Ibid., 144.
[38] Elder, *The "Hindered Hand,"* 89.

announces to white bystanders that he intends to surrender but would like to talk with the sheriff first. Gus calls the sheriff, the governor, the president, and a British legation, and they all refuse to protect him from the lynch mob that has formed. In response to white rebuffs, Martin angrily retorts, "I have telephoned 'round the world and there ain't no justice nowhere fur a black man. We'll fight it out right here."[39] Gus is later visited by Tiara, the sister of the man he murdered. She convinces him to surrender, but shortly after turning himself over to the police, he is shot and killed by a white mob.[40] Although Tiara convinces Gus to surrender, Griggs makes clear that Gus would have fought to the death (and killed some white lynchers in the process) even though he was encircled by armed whites. By endeavoring to fight back, Gus asserted manly courage and human agency despite the inevitability of death. In this way, Griggs highlighted Gus's courage and heroism without depicting Gus engaging in violence against white lynchers. Although Griggs abhorred violence (particularly as a means to garner black equality), Gus's failed attempt to get the state to protect him and his subsequent violent confrontation with the mob suggests that Griggs understood armed self-defense as a tactic of last resort. By the same token, Gus Martin's ignored appeals for protection from white authorities suggest that armed resistance might as well be the first response.[41] However, though Griggs might have conditionally accepted armed resistance, he did not glorify it. Martin, like every black character of the novel who violently resists white mob violence, is eventually murdered by whites.

The Hindered Hand culminates with Earl recommitting himself to ending racial oppression through nonviolent means following his foiled armed resistance plot. In part, his political reversal is motivated by the intense depression of Eunice Seabright, his wife, which was triggered by whites' discovery of her black ancestry. Earl places Eunice in a Northern sanatorium and commits himself to fomenting a plot that will hasten the demise of racial prejudice. Unlike his previous plot, Earl now employs traditional political channels. To do this, he assumes a white alias, he convinces Southern radical racists (particularly the governor of Mississippi)

39 Griggs, *The Hindered Hand*, 185.

40 Ibid., 190.

41 Cammie Michelle Sublette, "The Spectacle and Ideology: Twentieth-Century Representations of Lynching" (PhD diss., Southern Illinois University–Carbondale, 2003), 130.

to organize a virulent antiblack campaign throughout the North, and then he stealthily convinces Southern and Northern liberals to unite and oppose it. Although Earl successfully unites the moderate factions of both races to oppose racial prejudice, his wife remains convinced that racial intolerance will endure, and she falls deeper into depression.[42] Interestingly, by the novel's end, Earl is responsible for an improved racial climate in the South.[43] Earl's transformation is part of a trend in *The Hindered Hand* in which conservative characters (such as Ensal) coerce radical and moderate black factions to adopt a conservative political philosophy.[44]

Despite Earl's success in uniting Northern and Southern moderates in opposition to Southern extremism, *The Hindered Hand* concludes pessimistically. In light of black characters' expressed hope for white moral renewal, the novel's concluding chapters suggest that racial reform is unlikely; therefore, blacks ought to find alternative solutions. For example, Ensal loses faith in God and the American political system in the aftermath of the Bud and Foresta Harper lynching and Gus Martin's violent death. These developments dramatically undermine Ensal's faith in rational, nonviolent solutions to racial intolerance as well as the viability of white cooperation in that struggle. As a result, Ensal immigrates to Africa, which suggests that Griggs understood it as a place to which desperate people could return if every other political solution failed.[45]

In sum, Sutton Griggs's *The Hindered Hand* refuted racist representations of the lynched black body that white novels such as *The Leopard Spots* popularized at the turn of the twentieth century. In order to accomplish this, Griggs reframes white lynchers (even children) as taking perverse pleasure in gratuitous violence against black bodies. Through whites' penchant to lynch black bodies for any and all reasons, Griggs suggests that it is in fact whites who were racially, morally, and socially inferior to blacks. In addition, *The Hindered Hand* explores the possibilities and meanings of black resistance to white violence. Throughout the novel, Griggs suggests that blacks should eschew armed resistance in favor of interracial coalition building, for both pragmatic and ideological reasons. Griggs portrays armed resistance as futile

[42] Griggs, *The Hindered Hand*, 240–268.

[43] Elder, *The "Hindered Hand,"* 92.

[44] T. Harris, *Exorcising Blackness*, 80; Sublette, "Spectacle and Ideology," 132.

[45] Elder, *The "Hindered Hand,"* 93.

because whites had superior numbers, weapons, and training; therefore, black armed resistance would always be doomed to failure. More importantly, Griggs suggests that armed resistance would likely engender a white backlash and, consequently, endanger the possibility of interracial coalition building, which Griggs believed was a requirement for ending racial oppression. Thus, Griggs's *The Hindered Hand* portrays nonviolent political agitation and moral suasion as the only feasible options to oppose lynch mob violence. It is important to note that Griggs's discussion of armed resistance illustrates the extent to which militant action and rhetoric in response to white lynch mob violence had become the status quo within black discourse by the turn of the twentieth century.[46] Given this circumstance, Griggs could not simply dismiss black violent resistance; rather, he had to provide a cogent argument against it as a means of persuading a black readership that did not likely share his conservative politics or his abhorrence to armed resistance.

Despite Griggs's opposition to armed resistance, in two instances in *The Hindered Hand*, black characters come close to violently retaliating against whites in response to lynching, although in both instances moderate black characters intercede and stall it. Both Earl's and Gus's scuttled plots to kill whites allowed Griggs to highlight black masculine courage in response to white lynch mob violence without depicting a violent clash between whites and blacks. By hinting at black armed resistance but never actualizing it, Griggs remained true to his belief that the race problem should be resolved through peaceful means, while simultaneously illustrating that black people courageously embraced resistance to white lynch mob violence despite the inevitability of death. In doing so, Griggs's overarching point was to suggest that regardless of the approach, the violent murder of black people did not lead to black Americans submitting to racial violence, but rather it emboldened them to fight back. In other words, Griggs asserts that though blacks were victims of lynching, they were not victimized by it.

TO STAND AND FIGHT

Perhaps more than any other black writer of the early twentieth century, Richard Wright devoted his literary career to understanding

[46] Coleman, *Sutton E. Griggs*, ix.

how racial violence shaped black consciousness.[47] Although racial violence is an ever-present metanarrative across Wright's literary catalog, *Uncle Tom's Children* (1938), Wright's first major publication, delved deepest into black armed resistance to white lynch mob violence. *In Uncle Tom's Children*, Wright explored what it meant to stand and fight and/or flee lynch mob violence. Each of the book's five short stories' dramatic tensions revolves around how blacks (individually and collectively) should respond to white violence. Of the stories, "Long Black Song," "Big Boy Leaves Home," and "Bright and Morning Star" best illustrate how Wright used black armed resistance to white mob violence to construct consoling narratives of the lynched black body. Unlike Sutton Griggs, Wright portrays armed resistance as a legitimate and necessary response to white lynch mob violence. Wright's black characters consciously choose to stand and fight even though they know they will be killed by white lynchers as a result. With the choice to stand and fight, Wright emphasizes the heroic nature of black violent resistance to lynch mob violence as well as how black violent resistance signified how black lynch victims could overcome and even transcend the omnipresent threat of death that the lynching spectacle sought to inculcate in black Americans.

Richard Wright's "Long Black Song" is probably partially autobiographical, especially in terms of his family's abject poverty and his exposure to racial violence.[48] In 1908, Wright was born on a plantation outside of Natchez, Mississippi, to Nathan Wright, a sharecropper, and Ella Wright, a schoolteacher. Between 1908 and 1914, the Wrights shuffled between Natchez and Memphis, Tennessee, in search of better employment opportunities. However, Nathan abandoned the family in 1914; consequently, the Wrights' economic hardships increased significantly. In order to survive, Wright and his siblings were placed in an orphanage. By 1916, however, they had moved in with relatives, Aunt Maggie and Uncle Silas, a saloonkeeper, in Elaine, Arkansas. For a brief period, Wright and his siblings were lifted out of poverty, but after his Uncle Silas was murdered by whites who resented his

[47] See Abdul JanMohamed, *The Death-Bound-Subject: Richard Wright's Archaeology of Death* (Durham: Duke University Press, 2005), 1.

[48] Keneth Kinnamon, *The Emergence of Richard Wright: A Study in Literature and Society* (Urbana: University of Illinois Press, 1972), 4.

successful business, they narrowly escaped to West Helena, Arkansas.[49]

Silas is also the name of the main protagonist in "Long Black Song." In this story world, Silas is an industrious black sharecropper who is married to the enigmatic Sarah. The story's drama unfolds while Silas is in town selling his cotton crop at market. As with other black sharecroppers, Silas has long endured the exploitative sharecropping system and dreams of owning his own farm, which he expects to purchase from the proceeds of his cotton sales. While he is away, Sarah anxiously awaits his return because he has promised to bring her some fine cloth. Nonetheless, Sarah feels lonesome in his absence and fantasizes about Tom, her old lover, who has gone off to fight in World War I. She prefers Tom as a lover but reassures herself that Silas is a good provider. As she daydreams, she is visited by a white clock salesman. At first, Sarah and the salesman chat innocently; however, their encounter escalates when the salesman fondles her. She initially resists but seemingly relents to his advances and they have intercourse. Afterward, the salesman leaves a clock upon the promise that he will return to collect payment the next day.[50]

In the meantime, Silas returns home and happily relays to Sarah that he has sold his cotton for $250 and used a portion of the profit as down payment on ten acres of land. Feeling his fortunes changing, Silas exclaims that he will need to hire a laborer (like white folks) to help farm his new landholdings. Amid Silas's joyous return, he gradually discovers Sarah's sexual indiscretion, destroys the clock, and threatens to beat her and the salesmen with a horsewhip. Fearing for her life, she flees to a nearby hill, where she remains until the following morning.[51]

As expected, the salesman returns the next day. From the hill, Sarah observes the impending confrontation. As Sarah has feared, Silas angrily relays his disdain to the salesman and then proceeds to lash and shoot him. Silas then opens fire on the white man who has accompanied the salesman, who narrowly escapes and later returns with a lynch mob. Before the mob arrives, Sarah returns home and pleads with Silas to flee before the mob comes. Instead, he sends her

[49] Robert Butler, *The Critical Response to Richard Wright* (Westport: Greenwood Press, 1995), x.

[50] Richard Wright, *Uncle Tom's Children* (New York: Harper Collins Publishers, 2008), 125–138.

[51] Ibid., 139–148.

away and barricades himself in their house. When the mob approaches, he shoots several white men; in response, the mob sets fire to the house. In the end, rather than flee the burning house and submit to a certain lynching, Silas chooses to remain and dies in the fire.[52]

Prior to Sarah's betrayal, Silas believed that he could become equal to whites through personal sacrifice and hard work. In pursuit of that goal, he patiently endured the indignities of white supremacy. In so doing, Silas saved enough money for a down payment toward the purchase of a farm. He had plans to hire laborers to improve the farm and even restricted Sarah to household duties rather than fieldwork, which was typically required of black farm women. Silas believed that if he followed the "white man's rules," he could insulate himself to a degree from white oppression.

After the discovery of Sarah's tryst with the clock salesman, Silas felt betrayed by Sarah because she allowed the white salesman into their home and was sexually unfaithful.[53] Of the two betrayals, it seems that allowing the white salesman into their home was the most egregious. Furthermore, Sarah's betrayal destroyed Silas's hope that his individual strivings could stave off white supremacy. Upon this realization, Silas's repressed hatred of whites replaced his desire to be their equal. In one passage, he angrily scolds Sarah by declaring,

> Gawddam yo black soul t hell, don yuh try lyin t me! Ef yuh start layin wid white men Ahll hoss-whip yuh ta incha yo life. Shos theres Gawd in heaven Ah will! From sunup to sundown Ah work mah guts out t pay them white trash bastrards whut Ah owe em, n then Ah comes n fins they been in mah house! Ah cant go into their houses, n yuh know Gawddam well Ah cant! They don have no mercy on no black folks, wes just like dirt under their feet! Fer ten years Ah slaves lika dog t git mah farm free, givin every penny Ah kin t em, n then Ah comes n fins they been in mah house.... Ef yuh wans t eat at mah table yuhs gonna keep them white trash bastards out, yuh hear? Tha white ape kin come n git that damn box n Ah ain gonna pay im a cent! He had no bisness leavin it here, n yuh had no bisness lettin im! Ahma tell tha sonofabitch something when he comes out here in tha mawin, so hep me Gawd![54]

[52] Ibid., 149–156.

[53] For an alternative analysis of Silas's sense of betrayal that centers upon property relations, see Alexandre, *The Properties of Violence*, 107–112.

[54] Wright, *Uncle Tom's Children*, 143.

Silas's transformation is further emphasized by his violent confrontation with the white salesman. His first act of resistance to white supremacy occurs when he lashes the white salesman with a horsewhip. By lashing him, Wright suggests that Silas (who had considered himself a slave to whites) is now emancipated from being deferential to whites and now literally holds the power to exact revenge on them for various insults. Moreover, Wright's emphasis on Silas's desire to emulate whites and his embittered realization that his goals are impractical indicate that Silas's confrontation with the white salesman is precipitated by accumulated oppressions rather than from a militant consciousness.

Wright portrays the mobilization of a white lynch mob to avenge Silas's insolence as a matter of course and not a rare occurrence. Rather than flee an almost certain lynching, Silas chooses to stand and fight. Deliberating on how to respond to the approaching lynch mob, Silas sullenly remarks,

> It don't make no difference. Fer ten years Ah slaved mah life out t git farm free. ... Now it's all gone. Ef Ah run erway, Ah ain got nothin. Ef Ah stay n fight, Ah ain got nothing. It don make no difference which way Ah go. Gawd! Gawd, Ah wish all them white folks wuz dead! Dead, Ah tell yuh! Ah wish Gawd would kill em all! The white folks ain never gimme a chance! They ain never give no black man a chance! There ain nothing in yo whole life yuh kin keep from em! They take yo lan! They take yo freedom! They take yo women! N then they take yo life! Ahm gonna be hard like they is! So hep me, Gawd, Ah'm gonna be hard! When they come fer me Ah'm gonna be here! N when they gime me outta here theys gonna know Ahm gone! Ef Gawd lets me live Ahm gonna make em feel it! But lawd, Ah don wanna be this way! It don mean nothing! Yuh die ef yuh fight! Yuh die ef yuh don't fight! Either way yuh die n it don mean nothing ...[55]

By refusing to flee to the safety of a nearby relative's home, Silas chooses individual rather than collective resistance, which underscores his personal courage and manliness. As the mob arrives to lynch Silas, Wright contrasts Sarah's fear and subsequent flight with Silas's unflinching resoluteness to violently resist the lynch mob. In doing so, Wright suggests that individual acts of violent resistance (though arguably doomed to failure) require masculine heroism.

Although Silas boldly chooses to stand and fight, he comes to this decision reluctantly. At the end of the previous passage, Wright

[55] Ibid., 152–153.

implies Silas's reluctance to kill whites when Silas states, "But lawd, Ah don wanna be this way. It don mean nothing! Yuh die ef yuh fight! Yuh die ef yuh don't fight! Either way yuh die n it don mean nothing." Silas's momentary reflection illustrates how he was caught between what he wanted to be (a prosperous farmer) versus what the system of white supremacy made him be (vengeful and desiring to kill whites). At this moment, Silas is poised to renege on violently confronting the impending lynch mob, but despite his reservations, he cannot imagine how a choice to flee or a choice to fight will allow him to realize his dream of landownership in a white supremacist society hostile to black achievement. In this way, Wright reemphasizes the notion that violent retaliation against white supremacy emerged as a result of accumulated oppressions rather than black militancy. Although Silas seems to lament his desire to kill whites, his hatred of them blunts his remorse. In the end, Silas decides to be "hard" like them and make them "feel" the suffering that they had wreaked upon his life. Moreover, in making the decision to stand and fight, Silas is empowered because, through violently confronting and killing whites, he will for once be able to deprive them of their dearest possession – life.

In addition, although Silas's actions are suicidal, his underlying objective is not suicide. By standing and fighting, Silas gains control over how he is going to die. Through embracing his impending death, he liberates himself from the fear of white violence, which Sarah's flight represents. Therefore, Silas is no longer controlled by fear; rather, he masters it. And rather than fleeing his burning home, Silas remains inside and is ultimately killed in the fire. In refusing to flee – which likely would have resulted in a lynching – Silas once again denies whites the ability to define the meaning of his death.[56] Therefore, Silas's death is an expression of his agency. By denying lynchers the ability to violently kill him, Silas gains a measure of victory even in death.

Ultimately, Silas chooses armed resistance in response to the white salesman's intrusion into his home and anticipated white lynch mob violence. Throughout his life, he had accommodated white supremacy with the hope that one day he could be the equal of any white man. In order to achieve this goal, he works diligently and represses his hatred of whites as he gradually accumulates enough

[56] JanMohamed makes a similar argument in regard to Silas's decision to stand and fight rather than flee. See JanMohamed, *The Death-Bound-Subject*, 59.

money to purchase his own farm. However, when Sarah has an affair with a white salesman, his manhood is irretrievably violated, but more importantly, he realizes the futility of seeking equality with white men. In a fit of rage, Silas kills the white salesman. Rather than flee the approaching lynch mob, he steadfastly awaits their arrival and violently defends himself. His decision to eschew flight dramatizes his new understanding of white supremacy: "yuh die ef yuh fight! Yuh die ef yuh don fight!"[57] Essentially, Silas comes to believe that whites would always win no matter how much he tried. While Silas's dim view of black agency and its inability to alter white supremacy may reflect a defeatist mentality, it is more likely that his decision to remain is due to his desire to exert a measure of control over his life – even if that control occurs within the limited structures of white supremacy. Thus, by refusing to flee and engaging in armed resistance, Silas decides that he would be "hard" like whites, and in doing so, he would force them to recognize his humanity. More specifically, Silas knows he is going to die at the hands of the mob, but that does not matter to him. What matters most is to reclaim a sense of dignity, honor, and integrity of which he has been deprived. In Wright's "Long Black Song," then, armed resistance to lynch mob violence was not about actually defending or saving oneself. In Silas's case, it affirms his manhood and humanity, which he had strived to express through landownership but ultimately is forced to express through armed resistance.

In "Long Black Song," Richard Wright's understanding of the function and meaning of armed resistance ignores political concerns. Wright was much more concerned with the devastating effects white racism and lynching had upon the black psyche. For this reason, he suggests that blacks (particularly those who faced the threat of racial violence) could employ armed resistance as a means to reclaim the dignity and humanity that was denied them within the confines of white supremacy. Whereas Griggs eschewed glorifying armed resistance for political purposes, Wright portrays it as an empowering masculine/heroic response. However, despite the positive psychological ramifications of black armed resistance, Wright somewhat pessimistically suggests that blacks could only reclaim manhood and humanity through death.

In contrast to "Long Black Song," Richard Wright's "Big Boy Leaves Home" is a coming-of-age narrative that centers on

[57] Wright, *Uncle Tom's Children*, 153.

confronting lynching as a rite of passage from boyhood to manhood. Wright signals this purpose by naming the story's central character "Big Boy" – an uncommonly masculine boy, but one who is not yet a man. Big Boy's passage from boyhood to manhood is primarily conveyed through two violent encounters.[58] In each, Big Boy has to make a decision as to whether he will stand and fight or duck and run. In the first incident, three black youths (Lester, Buck, and Bobo) playfully attack Big Boy. Rather than submit to their superior numbers, Big Boy chokes Bobo into submission and threatens that he will break his neck if Bobo and the group ever attempt to gang up on him again. The second violent encounter is precipitated by Lester, Buck, Bobo, and Big Boy's decision to go swimming at Ole Man Harvey's water hole. To the boys' dismay, a white couple arrives at the pool, and the naked boys hide in the nearby brush in order to escape detection. Fatefully, they decide to get their clothes and run for it, but they are detected by Bertha (the white female), and she screams for help. Her husband Jim comes to her rescue. Jim immediately shoots and kills Lester and Buck, while Bobo flees to safety. Instead of fleeing to save his life, Big Boy violently confronts Jim and bests him in the melee. The altercation comes to a head when Big Boy refuses to surrender the rifle he took from Jim and instead shoots him. Whereas the other boys' initial response was fear and flight, Big Boy valiantly stands his ground as a man would. Wright underscores Big Boy's superior masculinity by framing Jim as a solider recently returned from World War I. In choosing to stand and fight Jim, Wright suggests that Big Boy has overcome his fear of whites.

After Big Boy kills Jim, his parents and members of the black community decide that his best chance to escape a lynching is to hide in a kiln along the road, where a black truck driver will pass the following day.[59] If Big Boy can survive through the night, he could be secreted out of town on the delivery truck. As Big Boy hides in the kiln, he is simultaneously filled with fear and rage and channels these emotions into fantasizing about killing members of the white lynch mob whom he believes he will ultimately have to confront. Big Boy thinks, "Why hadn't Pa let im take tha shotgun? He stopped. He

[58] JanMohamed makes a similar argument concerning "Big Boy Leaves Home" as a coming of age narrative. See JanMohamed, *The Death-Bound-Subject*, 48–49.

[59] For a compelling interpretation of Wright's kiln imagery, see Alexandre, *The Properties of Violence*, 91–95.

oughta go back n git the shotgun. And when the mob came he would take some with him."[60] Big Boy's reflections continue:

> Yeah, ef pa had only let im have tha shotgun! He could stan off a whole mob wid a shotgun. He looked at the ground as he turned a shotgun over in his hands. Then he leveled it at an advancing white man. Boooom! The man curled up. Another came. He reloaded quickly, and let him have what the other had got. He too curled up. Then another came. He got the same medicine. The whole mob swirled around him, and he blaze away, getting as many as he could. They closed in; but by Gawd, he had done his part, handn't he? N the newspaper say: NIGGER KILLS DOZEN OF MOB BEFO LYNCHED! Er mabbe they say: TRAPPED NIGGER SLAYS TWENTY BEFO KILLED! He smiled a little. Tha wouldn't be so bad, would it? Blinking the newspaper away, he looked over the fields.[61]

For Big Boy, fantasizing about killing whites is a cathartic moment. It assuages and displaces his fear of lynching and allows him, for a moment, to enjoy a "festival of violence" against whites rather than one targeted at blacks. Big Boy takes pleasure in the spectacle of black bodies killing white bodies because this spectacle would dislodge the heroic narrative of white masculine prowess and black victimization.

As Big Boy fantasizes about killing white lynchers, a white posse captures Bobo and prepares to lynch him near Big Boy's hideaway. Without being detected, Big Boy watches as hot tar and gasoline are poured on Bobo's naked body. Finally, a match is lit and Bobo's body is set afire. As fire engulfs Bobo, he screams and writhes in painful agony. During Bobo's lynching, Big Boy never looks away. Although Bobo is powerless to prevent his lynching, he refuses to divulge Big Boy's hiding place. By doing so, Wright suggests that Bobo chose to die on his own terms rather than those of the lynchers. For all Big Boy's fantasies of killing white lynchers, he chooses to remain hidden. In fact, Wright's black characters only resist when resistance is somewhat futile – when resistance will not result in saving their lives. In this way, Wright's black characters are not suicidal, nor do they behave carelessly with their lives; this in part explains why Big Boy does not attempt to rescue Bobo. The point here is that Big Boy comes to the realization that white lynchers are not invincible despite the fact that he is unable to act upon this new insight.[62] Within the

[60] Wright, *Uncle Tom's Children*, 46.

[61] Ibid., 50.

[62] JanMohamed develops a different line of argument related to Big Boy's viewing of Bobo's death. For JanMohamed, Bobo's lynching represents the evisceration of Big Boy's subjectivity. See JanMohamed, *The Death-Bound-Subject*, 51.

context of "Big Boy Leaves Home" as well as Wright's other short stories, resistance is about signifying agency rather than the preservation of one's life.

Wright's "Big Boy Leaves Home" is a story about the perilous passage from boyhood to manhood for black males. Big Boy becomes a man by violently confronting white manhood; as part of that process, he comes to the realization that whites are not invincible. Moreover, Wright suggests that white lynchers' power resides in their numbers, not in their underlying masculine prowess or bravery. Therefore, although Big Boy is powerless to prevent the lynching of Bobo, he can claim a measure of victory through this realization, which marks his passage from boyhood to manhood.

Whereas in "Long Black Song" and "Big Boy Leaves Home" Wright primarily portrays black female characters as mourners or desiring divine intervention in the face of the lynched black body, in "Bright and Morning Star," he inverts the stock characterization of black women as long-suffering victims of white lynch mob violence. Here, Wright addresses the ways in which black women were forced to demonstrate selflessness and courage in response to the specter of the lynched black body.[63] Through his protagonist Sue's characterization and her centrality to the lynching narrative, Wright breaks the invisibility that has enveloped the history of black female lynch victims and also undermines the assumption that the emasculated male black body was the only visible victim of white lynch mob violence.[64]

"Bright and Morning Star's" central plot revolves around a secret meeting that is to take place at the home of a communist organizer. The town's white sheriff is seeking the meeting's location and the participants' names for the purpose of raiding the meeting. Reva, the daughter of a white communist organizer, visits the home of Sue, the story's main character, in order to inform her that the sheriff

[63] JanMomahed intimates a similar point regarding Wright's framing of Sue. He notes that Sue's characterization is "the one major exception to the general pattern of Wright's misogynistic representation of all forms of femininity"; see, ibid., 73.

[64] K. Mitchell, *Living with Lynching*, 173; Evelyn M. Simien, "Introduction," in *Gender and Lynching: The Politics of Memory*, ed. Evelyn M. Simien (New York: Palgrave McMillan, 2011), 2–3. According to the authors of *Gender and Lynching*, at least 150 African American women were lynched between 1880 and 1960. In addition, for a detailed analyses of black female lynch victims, see Julie Buckner, *Mary Turner and the Memory of Lynching* (Athens: University of Georgia Press, 2011), and Feimster, *Southern Horrors*, especially chapter 6.

has discovered the meeting place and plans to arrest communist party members. Sue is to relay the information to Johnny Boy, her son, who in turn will inform his communist comrades that the meeting place has been found out. After Reva leaves, Johnny Boy arrives and Sue gives him the message. Subsequently, Johnny Boy sets out to inform his comrades.

In the opening passages of "Bright and Morning Star," Wright frames Sue, a widow whose two sons are communist organizers, as a concerned and protective mother. With one son (who never appears in the story) already in jail for his affiliation with communists, she worries that her other son, Johnny Boy, will be jailed or killed. However, as the story unfolds, Wright upends the masculine paradigm of bravery and self-sacrifice by subverting Sue as a patient and long-suffering victim of white mob violence. Sue is entrusted with confidential information that if divulged would place her son and his comrades in harm's way. The story's main drama then revolves around whether or not Sue will exhibit the requisite courage for safeguarding the information and the extent to which she will go to protect the life of her son and his comrades.[65]

The first test of Sue's courage occurs after Johnny Boy's departure: the sheriff stops by Sue's home to inquire about Johnny Boy's whereabouts. Sue refuses to divulge this information, and in response to Sue's insolence, the sheriff beats her mercilessly. Each time the sheriff strikes Sue to the ground, Sue manages to get back up and even mocks the sheriff and his henchmen as they attempt to beat a confession out of her. Sue's courage is amplified because she does not temper her tongue in the presence of white masculine authority. Her determination to get back on her feet after being continuously knocked down implies the hollowness of white masculine violence against black bodies. Therefore, through Sue's characterization, Wright deploys defiance and courage as characteristics of black women.

Unable to force Sue to divulge the names of communist party members, the sheriff leaves Sue's home in search of Johnny Boy. Subsequent to the sheriff's departure, Booker, a new communist party member and undercover spy for the sheriff, arrives and convinces Sue to reveal the names of communist members. Booker recounts to Sue how Johnny Boy has been captured and is being

[65] JanMohamed makes a similar point in reference to Sue's characterization; see JanMohamed, *The Death-Bound-Subject*, 70.

tortured by the sheriff because he is refusing to give up the names of his communist comrades. With Johnny Boy captured and possibly near death, Booker entreats Sue to tell him the names of communist party members so that he can alert them before it is too late. In her weakened state, Sue divulges the names of communist members to Booker, and only afterward does she realize that he is a spy and a traitor. Realizing her mistake, Sue goes in search of Booker so that she can kill him before he can relay the information to the sheriff. Up until this point, Sue had been most concerned with protecting her sons from jail or death. However, after Sue's unwitting admission, the story's dramatic tension transfers to whether Sue will be overwhelmed with motherly duty to find and protect her son or whether she will remain defiant and persist at all costs in her mission to prevent Booker from sharing information with the sheriff.

In the story's final scenes, Wright portrays Sue as a trickster who easily outwits whites and makes them accomplices in their own demise. After Sue leaves her home in search of Booker, she haphazardly comes upon the sheriff and the white search party that has captured Johnny Boy. Unbeknownst to the sheriff, Sue has concealed a gun underneath a white sheet that she is holding. Sue pretends that she will use the white sheet to recover what she believes will be her son's lynched black body. The sheriff ridicules Sue for bringing a white sheet to cover Johnny Boy's body, because she is unaware that he is yet alive despite being brutally beaten and tortured. The sheriff hopes that she will convince Johnny Boy to name names. When the sheriff informs Sue that Johnny Boy is alive and being tortured because of his refusal to name names, she is determined to kill Johnny Boy so as to spare him from torture. Yet Sue realizes that it is unlikely that she will be able to discharge two shots from her concealed pistol before being overpowered by the sheriff and the mob that has gathered to witness Johnny Boy's torture. At this moment, Sue realizes that she must choose between killing her son and killing Booker. Despite the gruesome torture of Johnny Boy, Sue refuses to divulge the identities of other communists. Given how Wright frames Sue as a protective mother in the story's initial scenes, it is expected that she would choose saving her son from torture over killing Booker and safeguarding the identities of communists. However, Wright employs this dilemma to illustrate the impossibility of black life and specifically the ways in which black women were forced to displace maternal instinct for the greater good.[66] By placing the safeguarding of communist party members' identities over saving her son, Wright suggests that Sue transcends her assumed motherly duty. By doing so, Wright amplifies Sue's courage and defiance. Moreover, even though Johnny Boy's beating renders him incapable of offering resistance, Wright nonetheless frames him as a historical agent because he does not divulge the names of communist comrades and therefore chooses to die on his own terms. When Booker finally emerges to relay the ill-gotten information to the sheriff, Sue unhesitatingly shoots him in the head, killing him instantly.

As Sue anticipates, the mob subdues her at once. In order to avenge Booker's death, the sheriff forces Sue to watch Johnny Boy's lynching, and afterward, Booker's friend kills Sue. Despite the vengeful pleasure whites derive from both lynchings, Wright suggests that the lynching was an empty triumph because both Sue and Johnny embrace the inevitability of their death and therefore transcend it. In choosing to conceal the identities of other communists, both Sue and Johnny courageously choose death. In doing so, they achieve a measure of victory in defeat. As JanMohamed notes, Sue's "peace comes from being more in command of one's own life at the very point of death."[67] Through Sue's characterization, Wright depicts the depth of black women's courage and, more importantly, challenges the idea that black women were helpless witnesses of the lynching of black men. In this way, Wright suggests that the lynched black body as a historical agent can be both male and female.

In *Uncle Tom's Children*, Wright's portrayals of lynching and the lynched black body revolve around demonstrating black agency through the torturous choices black characters were compelled to make in the face of white violence. For Wright, the dearth of choices available to black Americans signified how white supremacy constricted the possibilities for black selfhood. Black characters in *Uncle Tom's Children* rarely choose between life and death – they choose how to die. Even within their very limited options, Wright's black characters often offer resistance to white lynchers despite the fact that this resistance will not change the ultimate outcome. For Wright, the real significance of these choices lay in their rhetorical

[66] JanMohamed makes a similar point regarding the displacement of Sue's maternal instinct; see JanMohamed, *The Death-Bound-Subject*, 74.

[67] Ibid.

effects: the ways in which those decisions position black subjectivity for black audiences. By emphasizing the efficacy of black agency in the context of the lynching spectacle, Wright suggests that black Americans could claim a measure of victory even in defeat. Stated differently, African Americans may have been victims of white mob violence, but they were not necessarily victimized by it. In this way, *Uncle Tom's Children* consoles by underscoring the ways in which black subjectivity transcends the shadow of the lynching tree.

CONCLUSION

Beginning with Ida B. Wells's "Mob Rule in New Orleans," black writers transformed white-on-black lynching from a symbol of black death to a symbol of black empowerment. Black writers accomplished this by devising consoling narratives of the lynched black body that portrayed black lynch victims as violently and heroically fighting back against white mob violence despite the inevitability of death. Although black resistance did not prevent white lynch mob violence, consoling narratives emphasized that what was most crucial was that black lynch victims chose how they were going to die. In choosing to fight back and even take some lynchers with them, black lynch victims' violent resistance signified how they overcame the fear and powerlessness that white-on-black lynch mob violence sought to instill. In framing white-on-black lynching in this way, it was possible, then, to conceive of black lynch victims as heroic figures rather than simply as hapless victims. Even though lynchings were the pivotal dramatic moments in consoling narratives of the lynched black body, black writers suggested that the actions of black lynch victims rather than the actions of the white mob ought to be the crucial element in determining the meaning of white-on-black lynching for black Americans. Consoling narratives' emphasis on what black lynch victims did rather than what white lynchers did was about empowering black Americans to understand that although they were victims of lynching, they were not necessarily victimized by it. Stated differently, black writers devised consoling narratives of the lynched black body to make the trauma of white-on-black lynching bearable and to inspire black Americans to rise up against it. Yet although black writers were instrumental in reimagining the meaning of the lynched black body, the tradition of constructing consoling narratives of the lynched black body extends beyond

African American literature. Ordinary blacks who never composed a novel or short story also took part in this process in a variety of ways, such as remembering and telling stories. In Chapter 4, we will explore these narratives via an examination of black oral traditions.

4

Remembering Lynching

White-on-black lynchings were traumatic events for black Americans because of the pain and suffering associated with losing friends and family to terrorist violence. The remembrance of a lynching ensured that the trauma would be a recurring phenomenon.[1] Memories of lynchings or near lynchings could be so traumatic that black Southerners sometimes chose not to talk about them. For example, in an oral history interview in 2002, Carol Mosely Braun, the first female African American U.S. senator, recalled,

> There were a series of lynchings in Union Springs, Alabama ... in 1911. And I know that there were lynching[s] in that town and so the family – part of the family – left and went to Chicago. And frankly, I don't know, it's funny, part of the reason why what you're [HistoryMakers] doing is so important is 'cause a lot of that history people just didn't talk about it. Once something that kind of horrific had happened in their lives, they just didn't talk about it again.[2]

Echoing the same sentiments, Willye B. White, a black five-time Olympian and longtime Chicago resident, remembered,

> My grandfather was from Centreville-Woodville, Mississippi, and there was an occurrence there where either he was about to be lynched or he was – they

[1] Cathy Caruth, "Introduction," in Cathy Caruth, ed., *Trauma: Explorations in Memory* (Baltimore: Johns Hopkins University Press, 1995), 4–5; Kai Erikson, "Notes on Trauma and Community," in Caruth, ed., *Trauma: Explorations in Memory* (Baltimore: Johns Hopkins University Press, 1995), 187.

[2] Carol Moseley Braun, interview by Julieanna Richardson, March 19, 2002, The HistoryMakers, Black Studies Center, bsc.chadwyck.com.

were in the process of lynching him and he was able to break free. And in the process, the entire family . . . fled in the night, which was not uncommon for blacks . . . back in the apartheid days of, of, of America. So they fled. And these are things that I'm finding out now – it's something that they never talked about.[3]

The memories of Braun and White suggest that in some cases, black people opted not to talk about lynchings because it was too difficult or painful to discuss those horrific experiences – even with other family members. But whereas some black Southerners chose not to remember lynching due to trauma, others found ways to remember lynching in spite of it, and sometimes did so by creating less traumatic versions of those memories. These memories are connected with the tradition of consoling narratives of the lynched black body. Like black writers who emphasized the heroism of black lynch victims, black Southerners who constructed alternative memories of lynching acknowledged the trauma of lynching but chose not to dwell upon it. Instead, they centered their memories on the more consoling elements of white-on-black lynching. For instance, when black Southerners asserted that a black lynch victim was innocent of a rape accusation or recalled how a black lynch victim fought back, they deemphasized the actions of the white lynch mob and made the focal point of the story that of black innocence and black agency. Black Southerners also took solace in the fact that black lynch victims did not cower in the face of mob violence and instead fought back to protect their bodies and property. In these ways and others, deemphasizing black victimization and centering their memories on black agency and black innocence created not only a less traumatic version of lynching but also powerful stories of black empowerment and vindication.

In what follows, I examine how black Southerners remembered instances in which black lynch victims violently resisted white mob violence and lynchings or near lynchings precipitated by the alleged rape of white women. I draw on oral history interviews of black Southerners from the Jim Crow era, particularly from Duke University's Behind the Veil: Documenting African American Life in the Jim Crow South Oral History Project.[4] During the mid-1990s, the Behind the Veil team conducted hundreds of oral history

[3] Willye B. White, interview by Larry Crowe, July 2, 2002, The HistoryMakers, Black Studies Center, bsc.chadwyck.com.

[4] "About Behind the Veil," Behind the Veil Oral History Project, http://library.duke.edu/digitalcollections/behindtheveil/about/ (accessed March 15, 2015).

interviews of black Southerners across eleven Southern states. The Behind the Veil Oral History Project interviews provide a rich archive for recovering facets of black life during Jim Crow such as sharecropping, domestic work, attending church, and participating in fraternal organizations. More importantly, many African American interviewees recalled specific lynchings or near lynchings of acquaintances, friends, and family with candor and passion. Although there were certainly differences in how these individuals remembered lynching or the lynching era more broadly, the commonality of black experiences during this period facilitated the construction of a collective, empowering memory of white-on-black lynch mob violence.

MEMORIES OF INTERRACIAL SEX IN BLACK AND WHITE

Black Southerners transformed lynchings and near lynchings precipitated by white female rape allegations into consoling narratives by challenging the veracity of those allegations. In fact, black Southerners were in general deeply suspicious of such allegations. The 1903 lynching of a black man named John Dennis in Greenville, Mississippi, provides an illustrative example of black Southerners' skepticism of white female rape allegations and reveals the dramatic differences between black and white memories of lynching. For instance, white newspaper reports asserted that John Dennis actually committed the crime that led to his lynching – an attempted rape of a "well known" white telephone operator in Greenville. Reportedly, two hundred men demanded that the jailer turn Dennis over to them. When the jailer refused, the mob stormed the jail and used a railway rod to break into Dennis's cell. Subsequently, the mob took Dennis to the telephone exchange and hung him from a telephone pole.[5] Similar to the news reports cited here, white resident Lawrence Wade confidently recalled that a white telephone operator "was attacked by a negro man."[6] Ernest Buehler, another white Greenville denizen, recalled,

[5] "Lynching in Mississippi," *New York Times*, June 5, 1903; "Greenville Citizens Lynch a Negro," *Weekly Corinthian*, June 3, 1903.

[6] Lawrence Wade Thomas, interviewed by Roberta Miller, December 20, 1977, Oral History Project: Greenville and Vicinity, Mississippi Department of Archives and History, Jackson, Mississippi, 30.

There was a woman who worked at the Telephone Office. She was going to work, and a colored man grabbed her right across from Dr. Hirsch's Clinic there. And he dragged her off in that lot and they got to tussling and she got to screaming, and he started running, and he ran down Shelby Street. A mob formed and they located him down there in front of Joe Mauceli's store, up under a house ... and got him from under the house and took him back up on Nelson Street and lynched him on a cable there, a telephone cable.[7]

Taken together, white newspaper reports as well as white memories of the John Dennis lynching asserted without reservation or qualification that John Dennis raped or attempted to rape the white telephone operator. To be sure, Greenville whites' uncritical acceptance of John Dennis's guilt in part reflected white Southerners' embrace of the black beast rapist narrative (emerging in the late 1880s and gaining popularity in the 1890s), which portrayed black men as sexual deviants who desired nothing more than to rape white women.

In contrast with white press reports and Buehler's and Wade's acceptance of the rape narrative, black Greenville resident Florence Bailey's recollections of the 1903 Dennis lynching were skeptical of the rape allegation. Bailey asserted, "A telephone girl *said* [my emphasis] this boy tried to catch her and do something to her, and they caught him."[8] Bailey's emphasis on the "telephone girl said" does not reject the possibility of an attack; however, it strongly implies that John Dennis did not likely attack her. In casting doubt on whether a rape actually occurred, Florence Bailey implicitly asserted her belief in the innocence of John Dennis and implied that the veracity of the telephone operator's claim ought to be in question. As a consoling narrative, Bailey's subtle but incisive phrasing transformed John Dennis from a "negro rapist" as embraced by the white press and white contemporaries to a black man who was likely innocent of the crimes of which he was accused.

More broadly, black Southerners who transformed lynchings or near lynchings precipitated by white female rape allegations into consoling narratives typically avoided using the word *rape* and instead framed the subjects as black men "having dealings with,"

7 Ernest Buehler, interviewed by Roberta Miller, March 17, 1977, Oral History Project: Greenville and Vicinity, Mississippi Department of Archives and History, Jackson, Mississippi, 41–42.

8 Florence Bailey, interviewed by Daisy H. Greene, December 4, 1976, Oral History Project: Greenville and Vicinity, Mississippi Department of Archives and History, Jackson, Mississippi, 22.

"getting caught with," or "caught up with" a white woman. In explaining why lynching occurred, Mississippi native John Johnson simply stated, "These was just people you hear 'm say they'd been having some dealings with a white woman and these guys got killed."[9] Also, J. M. Williams, a black farmer and inhabitant of Yazoo City, Mississippi, cynically noted, "Well, they claim that he was a friend to a white lady. That's what they claim. Now whether it was true or not, I don't know and I haven't heard anybody else say they knowed, but that is what they claimed and they lynched him."[10] By emphasizing that a black man had "dealings with a white women," was "caught with a white woman," or was "a friend to a white lady," black Southerners implicitly suggest that black men were not lynched because they raped a white woman but, rather, because they had a secret relationship (sexual or otherwise) with a white woman. When the relationship was found out, the lynching of the black male followed, regardless of the circumstances. For example, Lawrence Wade recalled the lynching of a black man for fathering a child with a white woman in Greenville before World War I. According to Wade, "A negro who worked at the Hospital was lynched in the area which is now Strange Park. He was supposed to have fathered a child by one of the white nurses, and her brother and a mob chased him, when they found out, shot at him, and finally strung him up, on a low limb."[11]

Beyond simply raising suspicion of white female rape allegations, black Southerners transformed white narratives of white female rape into consoling narratives by framing white women rather than black men as sexual aggressors. For instance, Merlin Jones, who was born and spent his formative years in Canton, Mississippi, remembered one particular instance:

> There was another case in which a [black] man was killed because this [white] woman says that he had tried to have sex with her. But later on I learned that she said that if you didn't, she'd have you killed. One man said he did. He was afraid, but he said if he was going to die, he was going to be

[9] John Johnson, interviewed by Roberta Miller, April 28, 1977, Oral History Project: Greenville and Vicinity, Mississippi Department of Archives and History, Jackson, Mississippi, 91

[10] J. M. Williams, interviewed by Mausiki Scales, August 8, 1995, Behind the Veil: Documenting African American Life in the Jim Crow South, Rubenstein Rare Book and Manuscript Library, Duke University.

[11] Lawrence Thomas Wade interview, Oral History Project, 30.

guilty. He said it didn't happen one time, had to happen several times, and he eventually left town because he got scared. And so, it was strange how those people [whites] worked, how they lived.[12]

In another example, rural Arkansan Thelma Nash declared,

In those days, white women used to always like black men. And white men used to like black women. Don't fool yourself. And see a lot times a white woman, if a white woman was stuck on you and you went on and refused her, she could tell a lie on you and say you raped her or you tried to rape her just because she wanted you.[13]

Both Jones and Nash assert in their recollections that white women aggressively pursued black male sexual partners and used the threat of a rape charge to compel black men to have sex with them. If a black male evaded or denied a white woman's sexual advances, a jilted white woman could claim that she had been raped by a black man who had in actuality rebuffed her. As Merlin Jones's memory attests, black men oftentimes felt powerless to prevent unwanted sexual relationships with white women, and therefore they did the only thing they believed they could do – leave town. James Story, who was born and raised in Magnolia, Arkansas, recalled, "I have also known black young men who had to enlist in the Marine Corps and Army to get away from some white girl. He would have to leave or get hung, or get killed or shot."[14] As consoling narratives, the memories of Jones, Nash, and Story point to how white women – not black men – instigated interracial sexual encounters that precipitated lynchings. Their recollections forcefully make this point by recalling how a white woman's sexual advances could be so persistent that a black man had to take extreme measures to evade them. In this way, consoling narratives portray black men as the antithesis of black beast rapists by framing them as actively seeking to avoid sexual encounters with white women. Taken together, black recollections

[12] William Chafe, ed., *Remembering Lynching: African Americans Tell about the Segregated South* (Durham: Duke University Press, 2001), 19.

[13] Thelma Nash and Delores Woods, interviewed by Mausiki Stacey Scales, Behind the Veil: Documenting African American Life in the Jim Crow South, Rubenstein Rare Book and Manuscript Library, Duke University.

[14] Johnnie Williams, Mildred McKinney, and James Story, interviewed by Mausiki Stacey Scales, July 21, 1995, Behind the Veil: Documenting African American Life in the Jim Crow South, Rubenstein Rare Book and Manuscript Library, Duke University.

of white female rape allegations make a powerful case that white women were primarily, if not exclusively, responsible for interracial sexual encounters and the lynchings that typically flowed from them. Stated differently, Jones's, Nash's, and Story's recollections consoled by absolving from any wrongdoing black lynch victims accused of rape.

If Merlin Jones remembered a black man who capitulated to the sexual advances of a white woman because "he was going to be guilty" if she later revealed that he had "raped" her, Johnnie Williams's and Alma Thomas Hall's consoling narratives of white-on-black lynching reveal how white mobs knowingly attempted to lynch black men who were patently innocent of the allegations for which they were accused. To this point, Alma Thomas Hall, who resided in Greenville, Mississippi, for many years, recounted how her unassuming and innocent black grandfather was nearly lynched for appearing in public with his "white-looking" black wife.

Hall reflected,

> Grandmother was a very fair [light-skin complexion] woman. She was supposed to have been seven-eighths white, one-eighth negro. She had red hair and blue eyes and they lived on a farm. She would come to town once a year during Christmas with grandfather, who was a very dark man. My grandmother and grandfather took a wagon one Christmas Eve to town to shop and while they were there they were noticed by the people [whites] in the general store. They attempted to lynch grandfather, and she begged and begged. She had to get someone [a white person] who knew that she was not white to save his life. Of course, that kept the two of them from ever coming to town, to the point where my grandmother died because ... she got sick and died because she said she would rather die than to come to town with my grandfather because they would have lynched him.[15]

Hall's memory calls attention to how the near lynching traumatized her grandparents, yet the reason for recalling their experience was not to highlight their trauma. Rather, Hall's point was to illustrate how whites attempted to lynch and persisted in threatening to lynch an innocent black man whose only "crime" was to appear in public with his "white-looking wife." Arkansas native Johnnie Williams remembered an instance in which a white farmer caught his wife kissing a black tenant farmer. Williams reminisced,

[15] Alma Thomas Hall, interviewed by Daisy Greene, July 7, 1978, Oral History Project: Greenville and Vicinity, Mississippi Department of Archives and History, Jackson, Mississippi, 6.

You know what, a brother-in-law of mine, named Rueben Ratford ... he had a son that was working for an old rich white man in Louisiana and this white man had this big barn with horses and cows. And there was this old poor white man that was living on this same place, but this boy Rueben know what time to feed up, so he was down there feeding up and here comes his wife [wife of the poor white man] down there and she smacked [kissed] on him. He [Rueben's son] knew it was bad news in Arkansas and they'd kill you in Louisiana. The husband saw this and so when he walked up the hill, she hollered, he raping me, he raping me ... and he [the woman's husband] said naw you lying I saw it all. He said now what business do you have being at the barn anyway at this time of night, this is that man's job, why are you down here. You ain't got no reason for being down here.[16]

Despite catching his wife in a lie, Williams noted that "the white folks in Louisiana did not want to turn him loose after the husband told them that." According to Williams, the lynch mob eventually let Rueben Ratford's son go but made him leave Louisiana. Johnnie Williams's memory makes apparent that black culpability mattered little to frenzied lynch mobs, because any and all interracial sex (even when sought after by white women) between black men and white women had to be construed as rape. As a consoling narrative, Johnnie Williams's memory – particularly his emphasis on how the white farmer witnessed and attested to his wife's deceit – further illustrates how black Americans could take comfort in the knowledge that white-on-black lynchings precipitated by rape allegations were oftentimes the result of white female sexual overtures as opposed to black male sexual "deviance."

In sum, black Southerners who recalled with skepticism white female rape allegations or forthrightly challenged the veracity of white female rape allegations constructed consoling narratives of the lynched black body. In these consoling narratives, black Southerners made rape allegations that led to a lynching or near lynching less traumatic by displacing what white mobs did to black bodies or how whites portrayed black lynch victims as black beast rapists. Black Southerners asserted that white women not only consented to sex with black male partners but that they aggressively sought it. Moreover, black Southerners emphasized white female culpability in interracial sexual relations as well as white women's complicity in lynchings. In addition, black Southerners portrayed black men as innocent of rape allegations and highlighted this by recalling the extraordinary lengths to

[16] Johnnie Williams interview, Behind the Veil.

which black men went to avoid sexual encounters with white women. By flipping the narrative of white female victimization and replacing it with a narrative of black male innocence, black Southerners were seemingly able to take comfort in the fact that even though their friends and family were lynched or nearly lynched, they believed that they were innocent of the crimes they were accused of. All in all, the frequency with which black Southerners emphasized how white women fabricated rape allegations suggests that black Southerners were consoled by vindicating black men who were wrongly lynched for a crime they had not committed.

MEMORIES OF LYNCHING AND VIOLENT RESISTANCE

Black Southerners also transformed the trauma of lynchings or near lynchings of blacks into consoling narratives by centering their memories on how black people violently fought back against white lynch mob violence. Black Southerners oftentimes recalled how black lynch victims violently thwarted lynchings or killed whites who attempted to lynch them. As consoling narratives, these memories displace the actions of white lynchers and instead make black agency the focal point. In doing so, black Southerners made remembering lynching an empowering experience instead of a traumatic one.

For example, black Southerners transformed traumatic memories of lynching into consoling narratives by emphasizing the role that black violent resistance played in averting attempted lynchings. Mississippi native Leroy Boyd noted,

> At that time [Jim Crow era], if a [black] person had a little land, he had some kind of old gun around the house, see. Those type people wasn't afraid to speak up for themselves if they thought they was right, although they know that they could be lynched. Because I remember one of my uncles, he got into [it] with a white man. . . . The white man told his uncle that he was going to lynch him that night. All the negroes, they got their guns and stayed out at his house that night.[17]

Boyd's recollection is a consoling narrative because he frames the threatened lynching as a means of highlighting black community agency and empowerment. Instead of focusing on what whites intended to do and the fear that a threatened lynching incited, Boyd

[17] Leroy Boyd, interviewed by Paul Ortiz, June 22, 1995, Behind the Veil: Documenting African American Life in the Jim Crow South, Rubenstein Rare Book and Manuscript Library, Duke University.

chose to focus on how his uncle courageously stood up to a white man and how his uncle's courage inspired the black community to band together in his defense. In another example, Ms. Georgia Ford, a longtime resident of Elaine, Arkansas, recalled how her father killed white lynchers and escaped a lynching. According to Ford, her father told her and other children stories about the 1919 Elaine massacre, in which it is estimated that 856 black people were killed.[18] Ford recalled crying after hearing about how dozens of black men and women were hung during and after the Elaine massacre. Although Ford acknowledged the trauma of the massacre, her reason for remembering was not to recount trauma; rather, her main reason was to recall black agency. Ford displaced the story of carnage and despair by recalling her father's violent resistance and clandestine escape when she stated, "He killed a lot of white people and they [Elaine blacks] put him in a box and put him on a train and shipped him out of there. He said he rode the train until he got to the Mississippi River and he said he jumped off the train and swam across the Mississippi River."[19] Instead of simply a story of black

[18] The Elaine, Arkansas, massacre of 1919 was the most brutal repression of an agricultural reform movement in American history. The Elaine massacre occurred in the wake of a brief period during World War I when black sharecroppers enjoyed relatively higher wages and slightly better working conditions. In 1919, cotton sold for an unprecedented 85 cents; consequently, some black sharecroppers were able to net between $500 and $1,000 – an unheard-of sum for sharecroppers at the time. When cotton prices dramatically declined in the immediate post–World War I period, Mississippi and Arkansas Delta planters sought to reassert pre–World War I wage levels and work conditions. In response, black sharecroppers and tenant farmers in Elaine, Arkansas, organized the Progressive Farmers and Household Union of America (PFHUA) and planned to sue plantation owners for lost wages in 1919. Black farmers demanded better working conditions and higher wages comparable to those attained during World War I. In order to galvanize black agricultural workers, the PFHUA held meetings to recruit and educate workers on the cotton market and formed armed posses to protect meeting halls from anticipated attacks. Plantation owners in Elaine, Arkansas, mounted an extensive and organized campaign of violence against farmworkers because they believed that workers posed a grave threat to white racial domination and ultimately to their economic interests. In order to squelch the nascent labor movement, planters arrested dozens of blacks, assassinated prominent labor leaders, and murdered countless sharecroppers. Some newspaper reports even suggested that bombs were dropped on Elaine's black community. See Woodruff, *American Congo*, 74–109.

[19] Georgia Ford, interviewed by Paul Ortiz and Mausiki Stacey Scales, July 20, 1995, Behind the Veil: Documenting African American Life in the Jim Crow Rubenstein Rare Book and Manuscript Library, Duke University.

lynching, Ford recalled how her father killed numerous whites and outsmarted his would-be lynchers. Rather than terror, the memory of her father's violent resistance and escape allowed her to see the Elaine massacre as a partial triumph over white lynchers. Although whites lynched hundreds of blacks, Ford's memory of the Elaine massacre is a consoling narrative because she chose to remember it as a narrative of fighting back and survival. In other words, rather than focus on the eight hundred or more blacks who were lynched, Georgia Ford centered her memory on the one (her father) that survived through individual grit and collective effort. Therefore, Ford's emphasis on black violent resistance transformed an otherwise horrific occurrence into a story of triumph.

In another example, Arkansas native and factory worker Tolbert Chism reminisced about how a white lynch mob headed by the sheriff made an attempt to lynch his uncle Forrest Chism; however, black people were armed and ready to violently defend themselves. Tolbert Chism recounted,

> I can remember one time this story was told of this fellow that was supposed to be the deputy that lived in our community and his name was Clem Simmons. The whites had it in for some of the blacks that lived up in our community. And in particular this was an uncle of mine that was name Forrest Chism. Forrest was what they called half Choctaw Indian and then half black. But he was really a marksman with a Winchester or any kind of gun. They had gathered up a posse and had the sheriff with them to go and get Forrest Chism about something ... but I think everybody had been alerted in the community because everybody had the Winchester ... every black house in the community at one time had a Winchester in it. And the reason why they did that was a lot of those blacks came in from over there in the Indians in Tennessee. And so this fellow Clem Simmons was at the head of the posse the story goes ... he held up his hand when he got to a certain point and said ... now all those houses in the [black] community have a Winchester in them and Forrest Chism is the captain and he really knows how to shoot those guns. And he [Clem Simmons] said that I am really afraid to go over there and offend them because if we do, all of us will not be coming back. Now it's entirely up to you, if you want to go on with it, we can go on with it, but if you don't want to, we all can stay alive.[20]

Rather than a story about nearly being lynched and the fear that the attempted lynching inspired, Tolbert Chism's memory is a consoling

[20] Tolbert Chism, interviewed by Paul Ortiz, July 15, 1995, Behind the Veil: Documenting African American Life in the Jim Crow South, Rubenstein Rare Book and Manuscript Library, Duke University.

narrative because his recollection became a moment in which to highlight black empowerment through collective violent resistance. Chism accomplishes this by emphasizing that black people owned guns and were expert marksmen. Moreover, Chism seemingly took pride in the fact that black people were capable of violent self-defense and that they collectively banded together for that purpose. In addition, Chism emphasizes that the black community was not paralyzed by fear of a white lynch mob. Instead, it is Sheriff Clem Simmons and the white lynch mob who are portrayed as deeply troubled by the prospect of black violent resistance and fearful that they would be killed by militant blacks. As a result, Tolbert Chism could proudly recall how a white lynch mob was made to cower by the threat of collective black violent resistance. As a consoling narrative, Tolbert Chism's emphasis on black agency – and specifically black violent resistance – transformed the story of a near lynching into an empowering story of an averted lynching.

Whereas black Southerners such as LeRoy Boyd, Georgia Ford, and Tolbert Chism emphasized how black violent resistance averted lynchings, other black Southerners recalled how black wit and cunning could forestall a lynching. Daniel Swanigan, for example, reflected on his family's violent encounters with whites in the Arkansas Delta and how his family clandestinely escaped a lynching. Swanigan recalled that a white man hit his brother over the head and his brother "went crazy on him." A search party quickly organized, and he vividly remembered that airplanes circled above their family farm and the roads in and out of Wheatley, Arkansas, were blocked.[21] Interestingly, Daniel Swanigan's story is partially substantiated by a *Little Rock Arkansas Gazette* news report from January 1921. The report's headlines read, "Airplane in Hunt for Negro Shooter, Lynching May Follow Capture of Assailant of Wheatley Man." The report states,

> A negro, who this morning shot and perhaps fatally injured Russell Johnson, private secretary to H.K. Smith, well-known planter and president of the Rice Growers bank here, is believed to be surrounded tonight in the Big Creek bottoms, about three miles southwest of here, by a posse of about

[21] Daniel Swanigan, interviewed by Paul Ortiz, August 2, 1995, Behind the Veil: Documenting African American Life in the Jim Crow South, Rubenstein Rare Book and Manuscript Library, Duke University.

100 men. It is believed he will be captured before morning, and that a lynching will follow.[22]

According to Swanigan, his family weighed whether they could defend his brother against a white mob but soon realized that they had only two Winchester rifles and one box of ammunition. Instead of armed defense, the Swanigans secretly received assistance from the local sheriff (different from the sheriff noted earlier). Swanigan recollected that the sheriff said that "there was only one way out – dress that boy in women's clothes and get a police escort to get him out." Fearing that the sheriff would betray them, the family relied on their kin networks to secretly convey his brother out of Wheatley and across the Arkansas state line.[23] It seems that in the end, with white authorities and a search posse composed of at least one hundred men arrayed against them, the Swanigans outmaneuvered the lynch mob. Daniel Swanigan recounted a riveting story of clandestine escape. If his family had accepted the white sheriff's offer to assist in the escape, his memory would be a story of an averted lynching but not a consoling narrative. Swanigan's memory is a consoling narrative because it was recounted as a story of black agency. Because of this, Daniel Swanigan could recall with a sense of pride and triumph that despite all odds and without needing the assistance of whites, his family was able to avert the lynching of his brother.

In addition, black Southerners transformed otherwise traumatic lynching narratives into consoling narratives by proudly recalling how black lynch victims killed white lynchers. Mississippi Delta native Marcus Lucas explained that his family "did not take nothing off white folks." According to Lucas, "Big Mama was a great big old black woman and she was educated and man, she didn't take no stuff off no white folk and papa didn't either.... We have a reputation of treating folks right, but we don't take no stuff especially off white folks." Lucas's comments stemmed from his family's armed resistance to a lynching and subsequent forced migration from Amite County to Bolivar County, Mississippi, around 1903. He recalled, "They [his family] had an incident in Amite County, with a white guy. Big Mama's cousin was a Mr. Hood. He and a white guy was teaching school and it was

[22] "Airplane in Hunt for Negro Shooter," *Little Rock Arkansas Gazette*, January 9, 1921.

[23] Daniel Swanigan interview, Behind the Veil.

a math problem the white teacher could not work and he [Mr. Hood] worked the problem." Lucas remembered, "Mr. Hood told the white teacher that ya'll don't have the sense but you make all the money. . . . The next day they [whites] came to lynch him." According to Lucas, "They never listed how many white people he killed down there. They wouldn't even let them print it in the books down there. And the only way that got him is his bullet jammed up."[24] Lucas's memory is a consoling narrative because, although it acknowledges that his uncle was lynched, the main objective in discussing the lynching is to highlight how his uncle bravely and skillfully shot and killed many whites. In fact, Lucas seems to boast that whites were lucky to have lynched him and wouldn't have if it had not been for a mechanical mishap. Despite the fact that his uncle was lynched, by framing the lynching as a story of fighting back and killing whites, it was possible to remember an otherwise devastating experience in a way that evoked pride and empowerment. More broadly, Marcus Lucas's recollections made the point that black people did not sell their lives cheaply. Instead, blacks desired to kill as many lynchers as possible so as to exact a measure of retribution on white lynch mobs when possible. In discussing how some black victims of white violence desired to "take some lynchers with them," black Southerners suggested that white-on-black lynchings were not simply stories in which whites violently triumphed over blacks; rather, in some instances, they could also be stories of how black lynch victims made white lynchers victims as well.

CONCLUSION

For black Americans, remembering the thousands of black men, women, and children who were lynched by white lynch mobs has been a recurring trauma. To be sure, black memories of lynching were traumatic not simply because they featured brutal killings of blacks. Memories of lynching were also traumatic because these narratives hinged upon how white mobs victimized blacks. Black memories of lynching that told this kind of story are precisely what made remembering white-on-black lynching a recurring trauma. Yet

[24] Maurice Lucas, interviewed by Mausiki Stacey Scales, August 7, 1995, Behind the Veil: Documenting African American Life in the Jim Crow South, Rubenstein Rare Book and Manuscript Library, Duke University.

black Southerners who crafted consoling narratives of the lynched black body transformed these traumatic memories of lynching into stories of black vindication and empowerment. In the main, consoling narratives accomplished this objective by centering memories of lynching on black agency – what black men and women did to defend themselves, their loved ones, and their property from white lynch mob violence. Black Southerners recalled with pride how courageous blacks violently defended themselves against white lynch mob violence and in some cases killed lynchers in the process. These memories had the power to upend the narrative of black trauma and suffering. In addition, black Southerners transformed traumatic lynchings into consoling narratives when they highlighted the innocence of black male lynch victims who were accused of raping white women. Black Southerners who testified to black innocence took solace in the belief that their friend or family member was not the black beast rapist that white female accusers or white lynchers said they were. In the final analysis, by remembering black lynch victims in more empowering ways, black Southerners acknowledged the trauma of white-on-black lynch mob violence without letting the trauma define the narrative.

Conclusion

Since the 1880s, African Americans have made sense of the lynching of blacks in differing ways. Those understandings have ranged from conceiving of the violence against blacks as warranted lynchings, unwarranted lynchings, victimization narratives, and consoling narratives. Because black understandings of the lynched black body have evolved over time, the lynched black body is best understood as a floating signifier. Despite this varied history, the lynched black body in post–civil rights American culture is typically understood as a symbol of extreme white racism and black suffering. To be sure, this is one of the ways in which the NAACP and other black activists of the early twentieth century wanted Americans to engage with the lynched black body. The cultural staying power of the victimization narrative of the lynched black body is a testament to their decades of organizing. However, this understanding of the lynched black body is not timeless. This seemingly unmistakable symbol of black victimization and death at the hands of white lynchers was made to do other kinds of work, to convey other meanings – meanings that could actually affirm black humanity. Therefore, the lynched black body as a floating signifier means that the lynched black body in the black cultural imagination has been elastic enough to change with evolving political and cultural needs.

The ways in which African Americans have made sense of the lynched black body has been contingent upon a mix of political circumstances and cultural imperatives. As these characteristics changed, so did black-authored narratives of the lynched black body. For instance, when black vigilantes lynched other blacks because the criminal justice system ignored crimes committed against black Americans, black people believed that violent crimes such as murder and rape warranted lynching. However, as increasing numbers of blacks were lynched by white lynch mobs and whites began to justify lynching on racial grounds – rather than criminal deviance grounds – black people pivoted from embracing black vigilantism to condemning it. Moreover, in the late nineteenth and early twentieth century context in which the lynched black body had been stigmatized as black beast rapist, black Americans mobilized alternative narratives such as the victimization narrative. Black-authored victimization narratives portrayed lynched blacks as hapless victims of white lynch mob violence in order to counter racist depictions of lynched blacks as well as prevent lynchings in the making and help secure federal antilynching legislation. Even as victimization narratives were useful for certain political ends, they had limited cultural value for African Americans attempting to cope with lynching or affirm black identity. Black-authored consoling narratives' emphasis on fighting back transformed white-on-black lynchings from symbols of black victimhood and death to symbols of black empowerment and resistance. Consoling narratives caution us to remember that understanding lynched blacks as victims is not inevitable or always desirable. Rather than embrace victimhood, consoling narratives of the lynched black body illustrate how black Americans pushed back against understanding lynched blacks as victims, because doing so did not provide a means for black people to adequately cope with the trauma that lynching wrought. By rearticulating what the lynched black body meant to black people, black-authored narratives sought to strip away the power and potency of white supremacist narratives of the lynched black body. Whether through victimization narratives or consoling narratives, black Americans have crafted alternate understandings of the lynched black body for their own purposes and on their own terms. For this reason, the lynched black body could symbolize at one moment black victimization and at another moment, black heroism. In all these ways and for all these reasons, black-authored narratives of the lynched black body have shifted over time.

Lastly, in February 2012, unarmed seventeen-year-old Trayvon Martin was shot and killed by neighborhood watch volunteer George Zimmerman. In August 2014, unarmed eighteen-year-old Michael Brown was shot and killed by Ferguson, Missouri, police officer Darren Wilson. In October 2014, unarmed twelve-year-old Tamir Rice was shot and killed by a Cleveland police officer. These instances, particularly the Trayvon Martin shooting death, gave rise to the #BlackLivesMatter campaign, which has spotlighted how deadly force is disproportionately perpetrated against black people. According to the #BlackLivesMatter website, every eight hours, an unarmed black person is killed in America. In the same way that #BlackLivesMatter has sought to focus public attention on excessive violence against young black men, black-authored narratives of the lynched black body during the late nineteenth and early twentieth centuries had a similar import. Black-authored narratives of the lynched black body provided counternarratives to mainstream or official portrayals of black lynch victims. In mainstream narratives, black lynch victims were typically vilified as dangerous criminals or rapists who deserved lynching. Black-authored narratives that portrayed lynched blacks as victims or heroes sought to empower black Americans to think anew about the lynched black body. In addition, black-authored narratives of the lynched black body posited that black people were human beings that deserved the same legal and political protections as other American citizens. In today's parlance, black writers and activists who penned alternative visions of the lynched black body were making the case that lynched black bodies matter.

References

ARCHIVES AND MANUSCRIPT COLLECTIONS

Chicago, Illinois

Chicago Historical Society
Ida B. Wells Papers
To Save a Kinsmen Collection
University of Chicago Special Collections

Durham, North Carolina

Behind the Veil: Documenting African American Life in the Jim Crow South
Records, Rare Book, Manuscripts, and Special Collections Library, Duke University

Jackson, Mississippi

Alfred Holt Stone Collection
Federal Writers Project of the Works Progress Administration (Mississippi). Ex-Slave Narratives, 1936–1941
Henry Warring Ball Papers
LeRoy Percy Papers
Mississippi Department of Archives and HistoryMississippi Historical Records Survey, Historical Research Materials, 1935–1942
Washington County Oral History Project

Little Rock, Arkansas

Acts of Arkansas (microfilm)
Arkansas Adjutant General Records (microfilm)

Arkansas History Commission
Sid McMath Papers

Springfield, Illinois

Illinois State Archives
Papers of the Illinois Secretary of State

NEWSPAPERS AND MAGAZINES

Atlanta Constitution
Atlanta Daily World
Baltimore Afro-American
Cleveland Gazette
Chicago Broadax
Chicago Daily Tribune
Chicago Defender
Colored American (Washington, DC)
Commercial Appeal (Memphis, TN)
Courier (Connellsville, PA)
Crisis (New York, NY)
Daily Democrat (Greensville, MS)
Daily Picayune (New Orleans, LA)
El Paso Times (El Paso, TX)
Fort Wayne News (Fort Wayne, IN)
Galveston Daily News (Galveston, TX)
Greenville Times (Greenville, MS)
Indianapolis Freeman
Little Rock Arkansas Gazette
Little Rock Daily Gazette
Logansport Pharos (Logansport, IN)
Memphis Commercial Appeal
Memphis News Scimitar
Memphis Press
New York Amsterdam News
New York Times
Newark Daily Advocate (Newark, NJ)
Osceola Times (Osceola, MS)
Philadelphia Tribune
Pittsburg Courier
Richmond Planet
Times Democrat (New Orleans, LA)
Times Picayune (New Orleans, LA)

USA Today
Vicksburg Evening Post (Vicksburg, MS)
Vicksburg Herald (Vicksburg, MS)
Washington Post
Washington Times
Waterloo Evening Courier (Waterloo, IA)
Weekly Corinthian (Corinth, MS)
Weekly Panolian (Batesville, MS)

GOVERNMENT DOCUMENTS

Emmett Till Unsolved Civil Rights Act of 2007, H.R. 923. 110th Congress, 1st session. https://www.congress.gov/110/plaws/publ344/PLAW-110publ344.pdf

Senate Resolution 39. 109th Congress, 1st session. https://www.congress.gov/bill/109th-congress/senate-resolution/39/text

MICROFILM COLLECTIONS

Papers of the NAACP. Part 7, *The Anti-Lynching Campaign, 1912–1955*. Robert L. Zangrando, ed. Frederick, MD: University Publications of America, 1987.

ONLINE DATABASES

Ancestry.com: http://www.ancestry.com
BlackPast.org: http://www.blackpast.org
Black Studies Center: bsc.chadwyck.com
Historical Census Browser, University of Virginia, Geospatial and Statistical Data Center: http://mapserver.lib.virginia.edu
Lexus-Nexus: http://www.lexus-nexus.com
NewspaperArchive.com: http://www.newspaperarchive.com
Project HAL, Historical American Lynching Data Collection Project: http://people.uncw.edu/hinese/HAL/HAL%20Web%20Page.htm
ProQuest Historical Newspapers: http://www.proquest.com
ProQuest History Vault: http://www.proquest.com/products-services/historyvault.html

BOOKS AND ARTICLES

Aiken, Charles S. *The Cotton Plantation South since the Civil War*. Creating the North American Landscape. Baltimore: Johns Hopkins University Press, 1998.

Akers, Monte. *Flames after Midnight: Murder, Vengeance, and the Desolation of a Texas Community*. Austin: University of Texas Press, 1999.

Alexander, Ann Field. *Race Man: The Rise and Fall of the Fighting Editor, John Mitchell Jr*. Charlottesville: University of Virginia Press, 2002.

Alexander, Jeffrey C., ed. *Cultural Trauma and Collective Identity*. Berkeley: University of California Press, 2004.

Alexander, Shawn Leigh, ed. *T. Thomas Fortune, the Afro-American Agitator: A Collection of Writings, 1880–1928*. Gainesville: University Press of Florida, 2008.

Alexandre, Sandy. *The Properties of Violence: Claims of Ownership in Representations of Lynching*. Jackson: University Press of Mississippi, 2012.

Allen, Frederick. *A Decent, Orderly Lynching: The Montana Vigilantes*. Norman: University of Oklahoma Press, 2004.

Allen, James. *Without Sanctuary: Lynching Photography in America*. Santa Fe: Twin Palms, 2000.

Apel, Dora. *Imagery of Lynching: Black Men, White Women, and the Mob*. New Brunswick: Rutgers University Press, 2004.

"On Looking: Lynching Photographs and Legacies of Lynching after 9/11." *American Quarterly* 55 (2003): 457–478.

"Torture Culture: Lynching Photographs and Images of Abu Ghraib." *Art Journal* 64 (2005): 88–100.

Apel, Dora and Shawn Michelle Smith. *Lynching Photographs*. Berkeley: University of California Press, 2007.

Arellano, Lisa. *Vigilantes and Lynch Mobs: Narratives of Community and Nation*. Philadelphia: Temple University Press, 2012.

Ayers, Edward L. *Vengeance and Justice: Crime and Punishment in the 19th Century American South*. New York: Oxford University Press, 1984.

Baker, Bruce. "Lynch Law Reversed: The Rape of Lula Sherman, the Lynching of Manse Waldrop, and the Debate over Lynching in the 1880s." *American Nineteenth Century History* 6 (2005): 273–293.

This Mob Will Surely Take Your Life: Lynchings in the Carolinas, 1871–1947. London: Continuum, 2009.

Barnes, Kenneth C. *Journey of Hope: The Back-to-Africa Movement in Arkansas in the Late 1800s*. Chapel Hill: University of North Carolina Press, 2004.

Barr, Alwyn. "Black Urban Churches on the Southern Frontier, 1865–1900." *Journal of Negro History* 82 (1997): 368–383.

Barton, John Cyril. "'The Necessity of an Example': Chestnutt's *The Marrow of Tradition* & Ohio Anti-Lynching Campaign." *Arizona Quarterly* 67 (2011): 27–58.

Bay, Mia. *To Tell the Truth Freely: The Life of Ida B. Wells*. 1st ed. New York: Hill and Wang, 2009.

Beck, E. M. and Timothy Clark. "Strangers, Community Miscreants, or Locals: Who Were the Black Victims of Mob Violence?" *Historical Methods* 35 (2002): 77–83.

Beck, E. M., James L. Massey, and Stewart E. Tolnay. "The Gallows, the Mob, and the Vote: Lethal Sanctioning of Blacks in North Carolina and Georgia, 1882 to 1930." *Law & Society Review* 23 (1989): 317–331.

Beck, E. M. and Stewart E. Tolnay. "The Killing Fields of the Deep South: The Market for Cotton and the Lynching of Blacks, 1882–1930." *American Sociological Review* 55 (1990): 526–539.

"A Season for Violence: The Lynching of Blacks and Labor Demand in the Agricultural Production Cycle in the American South." *International Review of Social History* 37 (1992): 1–24.

Bederman, Gail. "'Civilization,' the Decline of Middle-Class Manliness, and Ida B. Wells's Anti-Lynching Campaign (1892–94)." *Radical History Review* 52 (1992): 5–30.

Benson, Christopher and Mamie Till-Mobley. *Death of Innocence: The Story of the Hate Crime That Changed America*. New York: Random House, 2003.

Bercaw, Nancy. *Gendered Freedoms: Race, Rights, and the Politics of Household in the Delta, 1861–1875*. Southern Dissent. Gainesville: University Press of Florida, 2003.

Berg, Manfred. *Popular Justice: A History of Lynching in America*. Chicago: Ivan Dee, 2011.

Berger, Martin A. *Seeing through Race: A Reinterpretation of Civil Rights Photography*. Berkeley: University of California Press, 2011.

Bernstein, Matthew H. *Screening a Lynching: The Leo Frank Case on Film and Television*. Athens: University of Georgia Press, 2009.

Bernstein, Patricia. *The First Waco Horror: The Lynching of Jesse Washington and the Rise of the NAACP*. College Station: Texas A&M University Press, 2005.

Bessler, John D. *Legacy of Violence: Lynch Mobs and Executions in Minnesota*. Minneapolis: University of Minnesota Press, 2003.

Bigelow, Albert Paine. *Europe and Elsewhere*. New York: Harper and Row, 1923.

Booth, Wayne C. *The Company We Keep: An Ethics of Fiction*. Berkeley: University of California Press, 1988.

The Rhetoric of Fiction. Chicago: University of Chicago Press, 1965.

Brandfon, Robert L. *Cotton Kingdom of the New South: A History of the Yazoo Mississippi Delta from Reconstruction to the Twentieth Century*. Cambridge: Harvard University Press, 1967.

Brown, Mary Jane. *Eradicating This Evil: Women in the American Anti-Lynching Movement, 1892–1940*. New York: Garland Pub., 2000.

Brundage, W. Fitzhugh. "The Darien 'Insurrection' of 1899: Black Protest during the Nadir of Race Relations." *Georgia Historical Quarterly* 74 (1990): 234–253.

Lynching in the New South: Georgia and Virginia, 1880–1930. Blacks in the New World. Urbana: University of Illinois Press, 1993.

"Mob Violence North and South, 1865–1940." *Georgia Historical Quarterly* 75 (1991): 748–770.

"'To Howl Loudly': John Mitchell Jr. and His Campaign against Lynching in Virginia." *Canadian Review of American Studies* 22 (1991): 325–341.

Under Sentence of Death: Lynching in the South. Chapel Hill: University of North Carolina Press, 1997.

"The Varn Mill Riot of 1891: Lynchings, Attempted Lynchings, and Justice in Ware County, Georgia." *Georgia Historical Quarterly* 78, no. 2 (1994): 257–280.

Where These Memories Grow: History, Memory, and Southern Identity. Chapel Hill: University of North Carolina Press, 2000.

Bruner, Jerome. "The Narrative Construction of Reality." *Critical Inquiry* 18 (1991): 1–21.

Bryant, Jerry H. *Born in a Mighty Bad Land: The Violent Man in African American Folklore and Fiction*. Bloomington: University of Indiana Press, 2003.

Buchanan, Thomas C. *Black Life on the Mississippi: Slaves, Free Blacks, and the Western Steamboat World*. Chapel Hill: University of North Carolina Press, 2004.

Buckelew, Richard Allan. "Racial Violence in Arkansas: Lynchings and Mob Rule, 1860–1930." PhD diss., University of Arkansas, 1999.

Buckner, Julie. *Mary Turner and the Memory of Lynching*. Athens: University of Georgia Press, 2011.

Burns, Adam. "Without Due Process: Albert E. Pillsbury and the Hoar Anti-Lynching Bill." *American Nineteenth Century History* 11 (2010): 223–252.

Butler, Robert. *The Critical Response to Richard Wright*. Critical Responses in Arts and Letters 16. Westport: Greenwood Press, 1995.

Callinicos, Alex. *Making History: Agency, Structure, and Change in Social Theory*. Boston: Brill, 2004.

Cantrell, Andrea. "WPA Sources for African-American Oral History in Arkansas: Ex-Slave Narratives and Early Settlers' Personal Histories." *Arkansas Historical Quarterly* 63 (2004): 44–67.

Capeci, Dominic J. *The Lynching of Cleo Wright*. Lexington: University Press of Kentucky, 1998.

Carrigan, William D. *The Making of a Lynching Culture: Violence and Vigilantism in Central Texas, 1836–1916*. Urbana: University of Illinois Press, 2006.

Caruth, Cathy, ed. *Trauma: Explorations in Memory*. Baltimore: Johns Hopkins University Press, 1995.

Cerny, Clayton Allen. "Reconstructing Freedom: Romance and Race in American Culture, 1877–1915." PhD diss., Northwestern University, 1996.

Chadbourn, James Harmon. *Lynching and the Law*. Chapel Hill: University of North Carolina Press, 1933.

Chafe, William, ed. *Remembering Lynching: African Americans Tell about the Segregated South*. Durham: Duke University Press, 2001.

Cha-Jua, Sundiata Keita. "'A Warlike Demonstration': Legalism, Violent Self-Help, and Electoral Politics in Decatur, Illinois, 1894–1898." *Journal of Urban History* 26, no. 5 (2000): 591–629.

Chamberlain, Mary and Paul Richard Thompson. *Narrative and Genre*. New York: Routledge, 1998.

Clarke, James W. "Without Fear or Shame: Lynching, Capital Punishment and the Subculture of Violence in the American South." *British Journal of Political Science* 28 (1998): 269–289.

Cobb, James C. *The Most Southern Place on Earth: The Mississippi Delta and the Roots of Regional Identity*. New York: Oxford University Press, 1992.

Cody, Cheryll Ann. "Kin and Community among the Good Hope People after Emancipation." *Ethnohistory* 41 (1994): 25–72.

Cole, J. Timothy. *The Forest City Lynching of 1900: Populism, Racism, and White Supremacy in Rutherford County, North Carolina*. Jefferson: McFarland & Co., 2003.

Coleman, Finnie D. *Sutton E. Griggs and the Struggle against White Supremacy*. Knoxville: University of Tennessee Press, 2007.

Corzine, Jay, James Creech, and Lin Corzine. "Black Concentration and Lynchings in the South: Testing Blalock's Power-Threat Hypothesis." *Social Forces* 61 (1983): 774–96.

"The Tenant Labor Market and Lynching in the South: A Test of Split Labor Market Theory." *Sociological Inquiry* 58 (1988): 261–278.

Crowder, Ralph L. *John Edward Bruce: Politician, Journalist, and Self-Trained Historian of the African Diaspora*. New York: New York University Press, 2004.

Crudele, Juanita W. "A Lynching Bee: Butler County Style." *Alabama Historical Quarterly* 42 (1980): 59–71.

Cutler, James Elbert. *Lynch-Law*. New York: Longmans, Green, 1905.

Daniel, Pete. *The Shadow of Slavery: Peonage in the South, 1901–1969*. Urbana: University of Illinois Press, 1990.

Davidson, James West. *They Say: Ida B. Wells and the Reconstruction of Race. New Narratives in American History*. New York: Oxford University Press, 2007.

Davis, Jack E. "'Whitewash' in Florida: The Lynching of Jesse James Payne and Its Aftermath." *Florida Historical Quarterly* 68 (1990): 277–298.

Davis, Simone W. "The 'Weak Race' and the Winchester: Political Voices in the Pamphlets of Ida B. Wells." *Legacy* 12 (1995): 77–97.

De Jong, Greta. *A Different Day: African American Struggles for Justice in Rural Louisiana, 1900–1970*. Chapel Hill: University of North Carolina Press, 2002.

Dickerson, Dennis C. *African American Preachers and Politics: The Careys of Chicago*. Jackson: University Press of Mississippi, 2010.

Dixon, Thomas, Jr. *The Leopard's Spots, a Romance of the White Man's Burden, 1865–1900*. New York: Doubleday, 1902.

Downey, Dennis B. "A 'Many Headed Monster': The 1903 Lynching of David Wyatt." *Journal of Illinois History* 2 (1999): 2–16.

Downey, Dennis B. and Raymond M. Hyser. *No Crooked Death: Coatesville, Pennsylvania, and the Lynching of Zachariah Walker*. Blacks in the New World. Urbana: University of Illinois Press, 1991.

Dray, Philip. *At the Hands of Persons Unknown: The Lynching of Black America*. New York: Random House, 2002.

Duggan, Lisa. *Sapphic Slashers: Sex, Violence, and American Modernity*. Durham: Duke University Press, 2000.

DuRocher, Kristina. *Raising Racists: The Socialization of White Children in the Jim Crow South*. Lexington: University of Kentucky Press, 2011.

Dyer, Thomas G. "'A Most Unexampled Exhibition of Madness and Brutality': Judge Lynch in Saline County, Missouri, 1859, Part 1." *Missouri Historical Review* 89 (1995): 269–289.

"'A Most Unexampled Exhibition of Madness and Brutality': Judge Lynch in Saline County, Missouri, 1859, Part 2." *Missouri Historical Review* 89 (1995): 367–383.

Edwards, Linda McMurry. *To Keep the Waters Troubled: The Life of Ida B. Wells*. New York: Oxford University Press, 1998.

Elder, Arlene A. *The "Hindered Hand": Cultural Implications of Early African-American Fiction*. Westport: Greenwood Press, 1978.

Ellis, Mary Louise. "A Lynching Averted: The Ordeal of John Miller." *Georgia Historical Quarterly* 70 (1986): 306–316.

Fedo, Michael W. *The Lynchings in Duluth*. St. Paul: Minnesota Historical Society Press, 2000.

Feimster, Crystal. *Southern Horrors: Women and the Politics of Rape and Lynching*. Cambridge: Harvard University Press, 2009.

Ferris, William R. *Blues from the Delta*. Garden City: Anchor, 1978.

Finnegan, Terence. *A Deed So Accursed: Lynchings in Mississippi and South Carolina, 1881–1940*. Charlottesville: University of Virginia Press, 2013.

Fisher, Walter and Robert F. Goodman, eds. *Rethinking Knowledge: Reflections across the Disciplines*. Albany: State University of New York Press, 1995.

Fitzgerald, Michael W. "To Give Our Votes to the Party: Black Political Agitation and Agricultural Change in Alabama, 1865–1870." *Journal of American History* 76 (1989): 489–505.

The Union League Movement in the Deep South: Politics and Agricultural Change during Reconstruction. Baton Rouge: Louisiana State University Press, 1989.

Foner, Eric. *Reconstruction: America's Unfinished Revolution, 1863–1877*. New York: Perennial Classics, 2002.

Foner, Philip Sheldon and Robert J. Branham. *Lift Every Voice: African American Oratory, 1787–1900*. Tuscaloosa: University of Alabama Press, 1998.

Francis, Megan Ming. "The Battle for the Hearts and Minds of America." *Souls* 13 (2001): 46–71.

Frank, Arthur W. *Letting Stories Breathe: A Socio-narratology*. Chicago: University of Chicago Press, 2010.

Franklin, John Hope and Loren Schweninger. *Runaway Slaves: Rebels on the Plantation*. New York: Oxford University Press, 1999.

Fredrickson, George. *The Black Image in the White Mind: The Debate on Afro-American Character and Destiny, 1817–1914*. New York: Harper and Row, 1971.

"For African Americans, Justice Was Often at the End of a Rope." *Journal of Blacks in Higher Education* 28 (2000): 123–131.

Freedman, Estelle B. *Redefining Rape: Sexual Violence in the Era of Suffrage and Segregation*. Cambridge: Harvard University Press, 2013.

Frisch, Michael H. *A Shared Authority: Essays on the Craft and Meaning of Oral and Public History*. Albany: State University of New York Press, 1990.

Gallicchio, Marc. *The African American Encounter with Japan and China: Black Internationalism in Asia, 1895–1945*. Chapel Hill: University of North Carolina Press, 2000.

Gatewood, Willard. "Arkansas Negroes in the 1890s: Documents." *Arkansas Historical Quarterly* 33, no. 4 (1974): 293–325.

"Negro Legislators in Arkansas, 1891: A Document." *Arkansas Historical Quarterly* 31 (1972): 220–233.

Gatewood, Willard and Jeannie M. Whayne. *The Arkansas Delta: Land of Paradox*. Fayetteville: University of Arkansas Press, 1993.

Geoffrey, Jacques. "Review of *Without Sanctuary: Photographs and Postcards of Lynching in America*." *The Radical Teacher* 59 (2000): 5–9.

Giddings, Paula J. *Ida: A Sword among Lions: Ida B. Wells and the Campaign against Lynching*. New York: Harper, 2008.

"Missing in Action: Ida B. Wells, the NAACP, and the Historical Record." *Meridians* 1 (2001): 1–17.

Giggie, John Michael. *After Redemption: Jim Crow and the Transformation of African American Religion in the Delta, 1875–1915*. New York: Oxford University Press, 2007.

Gilbert, Peter. *The Selected Writings of John Edward Bruce: Militant Black Journalist*. New York: Arno Press/New York Times, 1971.

Gillespie Michele K. and Randall L. Hall, eds. *Thomas Dixon Jr. and the Birth of Modern America*. Baton Rouge: Louisiana State University, 2006.

Gloster, Hugh M. "Sutton E. Griggs: Novelist of the New Negro." *Phylon* 4 (1943): 335–345.

Goings, Kenneth W. and Gerald L. Smith. "'Unhidden' Transcripts: Memphis and African American Agency, 1862–1920." *Journal of Urban History* 21 (1995): 372–394.

Goldsby, Jacqueline Denise. "The High and Low Tech of It: The Meaning of the Lynching and Death of Emmett Till." *Yale Journal of Criticism* 9 (1996): 245–282.

A Spectacular Secret: Lynching in American Life and Literature. Chicago: University of Chicago Press, 2006.

Gonzales-Day, Ken. *Lynching in the West, 1850–1935*. Durham: Duke University Press, 2006.

Gordon, Fon Louise. *Caste & Class: The Black Experience in Arkansas, 1880–1920*. Athens: University of Georgia Press, 1995.

Graves, John William. *Town and Country: Race Relations in an Urban-Rural Context, Arkansas, 1865–1905*. Fayetteville: University of Arkansas Press, 1990.

Graves, Tom. *Crossroads: The Life and Afterlife of Blues Legend Robert Johnson*. Spokane: Demers Books LLC, 2008.

Griggs, Sutton E. *The Hindered Hand: Or the Reign of the Repressionist*. Whitefish: Kessinger Publishing, 2007.

Grossman, James R. *Land of Hope: Chicago, Black Southerners, and the Great Migration*. Chicago: University of Chicago Press, 1989.

Gunning, Sandra. *Race, Rape, and Lynching: The Red Record of American Literature, 1890–1912*. New York: Oxford University Press, 1996.

Guralnick, Peter. *Searching for Robert Johnson: The Life and Legend of the King of the Delta Blues Singers*. New York: Plume, 1998.

Gussow, Adam. *Seems Like Murder Here: Southern Violence and the Blues Tradition*. Chicago: University of Chicago Press, 2002.

Hahn, Steven. *A Nation under Our Feet: Black Political Struggles in the Rural South, from Slavery to the Great Migration*. Cambridge: Harvard University Press, 2003.

Hair, William Ivy. *Carnival of Fury: Robert Charles and the New Orleans Race Riot of 1900*. Baton Rouge: Louisiana State University Press, 2008.

Hale, Grace Elizabeth. "Review of *Without Sanctuary: Photographs and Postcards of Lynching in America*." *Journal of American History* 89 (2002): 989–994.

Hall, Jacquelyn Dowd. "'The Mind That Burns in Each Body': Women, Rape, and Racial Violence." *Southern Exposure* 12 (1984): 61–71.

Revolt against Chivalry: Jesse Daniel Ames and the Women's Campaign against Lynching. New York: Columbia University Press, 1979.

Hall, Stuart. "Race, the Floating Signifier," https://www.mediaed.org/assets/products/407/transcript_407.pdf.

Haram, Kerstyn. "Pametto Leader's Mission to End Lynching in South Carolina: Black Agency and the Black Press in Columbia, 1925–1940." *South Carolina Historical Magazine* 107 (2006): 310–333.

Harris, J. William. *Deep Souths: Delta, Piedmont, and Sea Island Society in the Age of Segregation*. Baltimore: Johns Hopkins University Press, 2001.

Harris, Trudier. *Exorcising Blackness: Historical and Literary Lynching and Burning Rituals*. Bloomington: Indiana University Press, 1984.

Harrison, Hubert H. and Jeffrey Babcock Perry. *A Hubert Harrison Reader*. Middletown: Wesleyan University Press, 2001.

Hill, Karlos K. "Black Vigilantism: The Rise and Decline of African American Lynch Mob Activity in the Mississippi and Arkansas Deltas, 1883–1923." *Journal of African American History* 95 (2010): 26–43.

"Resisting Lynching: Black Grassroots Responses to Lynching in the Arkansas and Mississippi Deltas, 1882–1938." PhD diss., University of Illinois, 2010.

Hill, Rebecca. *Men, Mobs, and the Law: Anti-Lynching and Labor Defense in U.S. Radical History*. Durham: Duke University Press, 2009.

Hollander, Jocelyn A. and Rachel L. Einwohner. "Conceptualizing Resistance." *Sociological Forum* 19 (2004): 533–554.

Holmes, William F. "The Leflore County Massacre and the Demise of the Colored Farmers' Alliance." *Phylon* 34 (1973): 267–274.

Howard, Walter T. "'A Blot on Tampa's History': The 1934 Lynching of Robert Johnson." *Tampa Bay History* 6 (1984): 5–18.

Lynchings: Extralegal Violence in Florida during the 1930s. Cranbury: Susquehanna University Press, 1995.

"Vigilante Justice and National Reaction: The 1937 Tallahassee Double Lynching." *Florida Historical Quarterly* 67 (1988): 32–51.

Huber, Patrick J. "'Caught Up in the Violent Whirlwind of Lynching': The 1885 Quadruple Lynching in Chatham County, North Carolina." *North Carolina Historical Review* 75 (1998): 134–160.

Ingalls, Robert P. "Lynching and Establishment Violence in Tampa, 1858–1935." *Journal of Southern History* 53 (1987): 613–644.

Inverarity, James. "Populism and Lynching in Louisiana: 1889–1896: A Test of Erickson's Theory of the Relationship between Boundary Crises and Repressive Justice." *American Sociological Review* 41 (1976): 262–279.

Irwin-Zarecka, Iwona. *Frames of Remembrance: The Dynamics of Collective Memory*. Piscataway: Transaction Publishers, 2007.

Jackson, Lawrence P. *The Indignant Generation: A Narrative History of African American Writers and Critics, 1934–1960*. Princeton: Princeton University Press, 2011.

Jackson, Robert. "A Southern Sublimation: Lynching Film and the Reconstruction of American Memory." *Southern Literary Journal* 40 (2008): 102–120.

JanMohamed, Abdul R. *The Death-Bound-Subject: Richard Wright's Archaeology of Death*. Post-Contemporary Interventions. Durham: Duke University Press, 2005.

Jonas, Gilbert. *Freedom's Sword: The NAACP and the Struggle against Racism in America, 1909–1969*. New York: Routledge, 2005.

Jordan, Winthrop D. *Tumult and Silence at Second Creek: An Inquiry into a Civil War Slave Conspiracy*. Baton Rouge: Louisiana State University Press, 1993.

Kelley, Robin D. G. *Race Rebels: Culture, Politics, and the Black Working Class*. New York: Free Press, 1996.

Kermode, Frank. *The Sense of an Ending: Studies in the Theory of Fiction*. Oxford: Oxford University Press, 1967.

Kinnamon, Keneth. *The Emergence of Richard Wright: A Study in Literature and Society*. Urbana: University of Illinois Press, 1972.

Kousser, J. Morgan. "A Black Protest in the 'Era of Accommodation.'" *Arkansas Historical Quarterly* 34, no. 2 (1975): 149–178.

Kuhl, Michelle. "Modern Martyrs: African-American Responses to Lynching, 1880–1940." PhD diss., Bighamton University, 2004.

Leidholdt, A. S. "'Never Thot This Could Happen in the South!': The Anti-Lynching Advocacy of Appalachian Newspaper Editor Bruce Crawford." *Appalachian Journal* 38 (2011): 198–232.

Lemann, Nicholas. *The Promised Land: The Great Black Migration and How It Changed America*. New York: Knopf, 1991.

Leonard, Stephen J. *Lynching in Colorado, 1859–1919*. Boulder: University Press of Colorado, 2002.

Lewis, Todd E. "Mob Justice in the 'American Congo': 'Judge Lynch' in Arkansas during the Decade After World War I." *Arkansas Historical Quarterly* 52 (1993): 156–184.

Lin, Nan. *Social Capital: A Theory of Social Structure and Action*. New York: Cambridge University Press, 2001.

Litwack, Leon F. *Trouble in Mind: Black Southerners in the Age of Jim Crow*. New York: Knopf, 1998.

Lomax, Alan. *The Land Where the Blues Began*. New York: Pantheon, 1993.

Madison, James H. *A Lynching in the Heartland: Race and Memory in America*. New York: Palgrave, 2001.

Markovitz, Jonathan. *Legacies of Lynching: Racial Violence and Memory*. Minneapolis: University of Minnesota Press, 2004.

Massey, James L. and Martha A. Myers. "Patterns of Repressive Social Control in Post-Reconstruction Georgia, 1882–1935." *Social Forces* 68 (1989): 458–488.

McCoyer, Michael. "'Rough Mens' in 'the Toughest Places I Ever Seen': The Construction and Ramifications of Black Masculine Identity in the Mississippi Delta's Levee Camps, 1900–1935." *International Labor and Working-Class History* 69 (2006): 57–80.

McCurry, Linda O. *To Keep the Waters Troubled: The Life of Ida B. Wells*. New York: Oxford University Press, 2000.

McGovern, James R. *Anatomy of a Lynching: The Killing of Claude Neal*. Baton Rouge: Louisiana State University Press, 1982.

McMillen, Neil R. *Dark Journey: Black Mississippians in the Age of Jim Crow*. Urbana: University of Illinois, 1990.

Mehlman, Jeffery. "The 'Floating Signifier': From Levi-Strauss to Lacan." *Yale French Studies* 48 (1972): 10–37.

Mikkelson, Vincent P. "Fighting for Sergeant Caldwell: The NAACP Campaign against 'Legal' Lynching after World War I." *Journal of African American History* 94 (2009): 464–486.

Miller, Jason W. *Langston Hughes and American Lynching Culture*. Gainesville: University Press of Florida, 2011.

Mitchell, J. *The Strangest Fruit: Forgotten Black-on-Black Lynchings in America, 1835–1935*. San Bernardino: CreateSpace Independent Publishing, 2010.

Mitchell, Koritha Ann. "'A Different Kind of Strange Fruit': Lynching Drama, African American Identity, and US Culture, 1890–1935." PhD diss., University of Maryland, 2006.

Living with Lynching: African American Plays, Performance, and Citizenship, 1890–1930. Urbana: University of Illinois Press, 2011.

Moneyhon, Carl H. "Black Politics in Arkansas during the Gilded Age, 1876–1900." *Arkansas Historical Quarterly* 44 (1985): 222–245.

Moses, Wilson J. "Literary Garveyism: The Novels of Reverend Sutton E. Griggs." *Pylon* 40 (1979): 203–216.

Moye, J. Todd. *Let the People Decide: Black Freedom and White Resistance Movements in Sunflower County, Mississippi, 1945–1986*. Chapel Hill: University of North Carolina Press, 2004.

Muhammad, Khalil G. *The Condemnation of Blackness: Race, Crime, and the Making of Modern Urban America*. Cambridge: Harvard University Press, 2010.

Mullane, Deirdre. *Crossing the Danger Water: Three Hundred Years of African-American Writing*. New York: Anchor Books, 1993.

Olzak, Susan. "The Political Context of Competition: Lynching and Urban Racial Violence, 1882–1914." *Social Forces* 69 (1990): 395–421.

Orr, Marion. *Black Social Capital: The Politics of School Reform in Baltimore, 1986–1998*. Lawrence: University Press of Kansas, 1999.

Otto, John Solomon. *The Final Frontiers, 1880–1930: Settling the Southern Bottomlands*. Westport: Greenwood Press, 1999.

Pearson, Barry Lee and Bill McCulloch, eds. *Robert Johnson: Lost and Found*. Urbana: University of Illinois Press, 2003.

Perloff, Richard M. "The Press and Lynchings of African Americans." *Journal of Black Studies* 30 (2000): 315–330.

Perman, Michael. *Struggle for Mastery: Disfranchisement in the South, 1888–1908*. Chapel Hill: University of North Carolina Press, 2001.

Pfeifer, Michael J. "Iowa's Last Lynching: The Charles City Mob of 1907 and Iowa Progressivism." *Annals of Iowa* 53 (1994): 305–328.

"The Northern United States and the Genesis of Racial Lynching: The Lynching of African Americans in the Civil War Era." *Journal of American History* 97 (2010): 621–635.

The Roots of Rough Justice: Origins of American Lynching. Urbana: University of Illinois Press, 2011.

Rough Justice: Lynching and American Society, 1874–1947. Urbana: University of Illinois Press, 2006.

Phelan, James. *Experiencing Fiction: Judgments, Progressions, and the Rhetorical Theory of Narrative*. Columbus: Ohio State University Press, 2007.

Narrative as Rhetoric: Techniques, Audiences, Ethics, and Ideology. Columbus: Ohio State University Press, 1996.

Phillips, David. "Review of *Without Sanctuary: Photographs and Postcards of Lynching in America*." *Journal of American History* 88 (2001): 319–320.

Pollack, Harriet and Christopher Mettress, eds. *Emmett Till in Literary Memory and Imagination*. Baton Rouge: Louisiana State University Press, 2008.

Potter, Vilma R. *A Reference Guide to Afro-American Publications and Editors, 1827–1946*. Ames: Iowa State University Press, 1993.

Rable, George C. "The South and the Politics of Anti-lynching Legislation, 1920–1940." *Journal of Southern History* 51 (1985): 201–220.

Raboteau, Albert J. *Slave Religion: The Invisible Institution in Antebellum America*. New York: Oxford University Press, 2004.

Raiford, Leigh. *Imprisoned in a Luminous Glare: Photography and the African American Freedom Struggle*. Chapel Hill: University of North Carolina Press, 2011.

Rampersad, Arnold and David Roessel, eds. *The Collected Poems of Langston Hughes*. New York: Random House, 1994.

Raper, Arthur Franklin and Southern Commission on the Study of Lynching. *The Tragedy of Lynching*. Chapel Hill: University of North Carolina Press, 1933.

Rice, Anne P., ed. *Witnessing Lynching: American Writers Respond*. New Brunswick: Rutgers University Press, 2003.

Rise, Eric W. "Race, Rape, and Radicalism: The Case of the Martinsville Seven, 1949–1951." *Journal of Southern History* 58 (1992): 461–490.

Roberts, John. *From Trickster to Badman: The Black Folk Hero in Slavery and Freedom*. Philadelphia: University of Pennsylvania Press, 1989.

Roediger, David R. *Wages of Whiteness: Race and the Making of the American Working Class*. New York: Verso, 2007.

Royce, Edward. *The Origins of Southern Sharecropping*. Philadelphia: Temple University Press, 1993.

Rushdy, Ashraf H. A. *American Lynching*. New Haven: Yale University Press, 2012.

The End of American Lynching. New Brunswick: Rutgers University Press, 2012.

Russell, Margaret M. "Reopening the Emmett Till Case: Lessons and Challenges for Critical Race Prejudice." *Fordham Law Review* 73 (2005): 2101–2132.

Sackheim, Eric and Jonathan Shahn, eds. *The Blues Line: Blues Lyrics from Leadbelly to Muddy Waters*. New York: Thunder's Mouth Press, 2004.

Saikku, Mikko. *This Delta, This Land: An Environmental History of the Yazoo-Mississippi Floodplain*. Athens: University of Georgia Press, 2005.

Schechter, Patricia Ann. *Ida B. Wells and American Reform, 1880–1930*. Chapel Hill: University of North Carolina Press, 2001.

Schroeder, Patricia R. *Robert Johnson, Mythmaking, and Contemporary American Culture. Music in American Life*. Urbana: University of Illinois Press, 2004.

Schultz, Mark. *The Rural Face of White Supremacy: Beyond Jim Crow*. Urbana: University of Illinois Press, 2007.

Schwabauer, Barbara A. "The Emmett Till Unsolved Civil Rights Act: The Cold Case of Racism in the Criminal Justice System." *Ohio State Law Journal* 71 (2010): 653–698.

Scott, James C. *Domination and the Arts of Resistance: Hidden Transcripts*. New Haven: Yale University Press, 1990.

Weapons of the Weak: Everyday Forms of Peasant Resistance. New Haven: Yale University Press, 1985.

Seay, Geraldine Hord. "The Literature of Jim Crow: Call and Response." PhD diss., University of Florida, 1996.

Seraille, William. *Bruce Grit: Black Nationalist Writings of John Edward Bruce*. Knoxville: University of Tennessee Press, 2003.

Shapiro, Herbert. *White Violence and Black Response: From Reconstruction to Montgomery*. Amherst: University of Massachusetts Press, 1988.

Simien, Evelyn M., ed. *Gender and Lynching: The Politics of Memory*. New York: Palgrave Macmillan, 2011.

Smead, Howard. *Blood Justice: The Lynching of Mack Charles Parker*. New York: Oxford University Press, 1986.

Smith, Albert C. "Southern Violence Reconsidered: Arson as Protest in Black-Belt Georgia, 1865–1910." *Journal of Southern History* 51 (1985): 527–564.

Snyder, Robert E. "Daytona Beach: A Closed Society." *Florida Historical Quarterly* 81, no. 2 (2002): 155–185.

"Without Sanctuary: An American Holocaust?" *Southern Quarterly* 39 (2001): 162–171.

Sommerville, Diane Miller. *Rape & Race in the Nineteenth-Century South*. Chapel Hill: University of North Carolina Press, 2004.

SoRelle, James M. "'The Waco Horror': The Lynching of Jesse Washington." *Southwestern Historical Quarterly* 86 (1983): 517–536.

Soule, Sarah A. "Populism and Black Lynching in Georgia, 1890–1900." *Social Forces* 71 (1992): 431–449.

Stovel, Katherine. "Local Sequential Patterns: The Structure of Lynching in the Deep South, 1882–1930." *Social Forces* 79 (2001): 843–880.

Sublette, Cammie Michelle. "The Spectacle and Ideology: Twentieth-Century Representations of Lynching." PhD diss., Southern Illinois University–Carbondale, 2003.

Thames Leonard, Latonya. "Veneer of Civilization: Southern Lynching, Memory, and African-American Identity, 1882–1940." PhD diss., University of Mississippi, 2006.

Thompson, Julius E. *Black Life in Mississippi: Essays on Political, Social, and Cultural Studies in a Deep South State*. Lanham: University Press of America, 2001.

The Black Press in Mississippi, 1865–1985. Gainesville: University Press of Florida, 1993.

Lynchings in Mississippi: A History, 1865–1965. Jefferson.: McFarland & Company, 2007.

Thornborough, Emma Lou. *T. Thomas Fortune: Militant Journalist*. Chicago: University of Chicago Press, 1972.

Tolnay, Stewart E. and E. M. Beck. *A Festival of Violence: An Analysis of Southern Lynchings, 1882–1930*. Urbana: University of Illinois Press, 1995.

"Racial Violence and Black Migration in the American South, 1910 to 1930." *American Sociological Review* 57 (1992): 103–116.

Tolnay, Stewart E., E. M. Beck, and James L. Massey. "Black Lynchings: The Power Threat Hypothesis Revisited." *Social Forces* 67 (1989): 605–623.

Tolnay, Stewart E., Glenn Deane, and E. M. Beck. "Vicarious Violence: Spatial Effects on Southern Lynchings, 1890–1919." *American Journal of Sociology* 102 (1996): 788–815.

Trotter, Joe William. *The African American Experience*. Boston: Houghton Mifflin, 2001.

Umoja, Akinyele Kambon. "Eye for an Eye: The Role of Armed Resistance in the Mississippi Freedom Movement." PhD diss., Emory University, 1997.

"'We Will Shoot Back': The Natchez Model and Paramilitary Organization in the Mississippi Freedom Movement." *Journal of Black Studies* 32 (2002): 271–294.

Vandiver, Margaret. *Legal Punishment: Lynchings and Legal Executions in the South*. New Brunswick: Rutgers University Press, 2006.

Vinikas, Vincent. "Specters in the Past: The Saint Charles, Arkansas, Lynching of 1904 and the Limits of Historical Inquiry." *Journal of Southern History* 65 (1999): 535–564.

Wald, Elijah. *Escaping the Delta: Robert Johnson and the Invention of the Blues*. New York: Amistad, 2004.

Waldrep, Christopher. *African Americans Confront Lynching: Strategies of Resistance from the Civil War to the Civil Rights Era*. Lanham: Rowman & Littlefield, 2009.

Lynching in America: A History in Documents. New York: New York University Press, 2006.

The Many Faces of Judge Lynch: Extralegal Violence and Punishment in America. New York: Palgrave Macmillan, 2002.

Roots of Disorder: Race and Criminal Justice in the American South, 1817–80. Urbana: University of Illinois Press, 1998.

"War of Words: The Controversy over the Definition of Lynching, 1899–1940." *Journal of Southern History* 66 (2000): 75–100.

"Women, the Civil War, and Legal Culture in Vicksburg, Mississippi." *Journal of Mississippi History* 61 (1999): 137–147.

Waldrep, Christopher and William Carrigan, eds. *Swift to Wrath: Lynching in Global Historical Perspective*. Charlottesville: University of Virginia Press, 2013.

Watson, Martha. "Mary Church Terrell vs. Thomas Nelson Page: Gender, Race, and Class in Anti-Lynching Rhetoric." *Rhetoric and Public Affairs* 12 (2009): 65–90.

Wells-Barnett, Ida B. and Patricia Hill Collins. *On Lynchings*. Amherst: Humanity Books, 2002.

Wells-Barnett, Ida B. and Miriam Decosta-Willis. *The Memphis Diary of Ida B. Wells: An Intimate Portrait of the Activist as a Young Woman*. Boston: Beacon Press, 1995.

Wells-Barnett, Ida B. and Alfreda Duster. *Crusade for Justice: The Autobiography of Ida B. Wells*. Chicago: University of Chicago Press, 1970.

Wells-Barnett, Ida B. and Jacqueline Jones Royster. *Southern Horrors and Other Writings: The Anti-Lynching Campaign of Ida B. Wells, 1892–1900*. Boston: Bedford Books, 1997.

Wharton, Vernon Lane. *The Negro in Mississippi, 1865–1890*. Westport: Greenwood Press, 1965.

White, Hayden. *The Content of the Form: Narrative Discourse and Historical Representation*. Baltimore: Johns Hopkins University, 1990.

Figural Realism: Studies in the Mimesis Effect. Baltimore: Johns Hopkins University Press, 1999.

Wiegman, Robyn. "The Anatomy of Lynching." *Journal of the History of Sexuality* 3 (1993): 445–467.

Williams, Kidada E. *They Left Great Marks on Me: African American Testimonies of Racial Violence from Emancipation to World War I*. New York: New York University Press, 2012.

Williams, Yohuru. "Permission to Hate: Delaware, Lynching, and the Culture of Violence in America." *Journal of Black Studies* 32 (2001): 3–29.

"A Tragedy with a Happy Ending? The Lynching of George White in History and Memory." *Pennsylvania History* 72 (2005): 292–304.

Williamson, Joel. *The Crucible of Race: Black-White Relations in the American South since Emancipation*. New York: Oxford University Press, 1984.

"Wounds Not Scars: Lynching, the National Conscience, and the American Historian." *Journal of American History* 83 (1997): 1221–1253.

Willis, John. *Forgotten Time: The Yazoo-Mississippi Delta after the Civil War*. Charlottesville: University of Virginia Press, 2000.

Wolf, Charlotte. "Constructions of a Lynching." *Sociological Inquiry* 62 (1992): 83–97.

Wolters, Wendy. "Without Sanctuary: Bearing Witness, Bearing Witness." *JAC* 24 (2004): 399–425.

Wood, Amy Louise. *Lynching and Spectacle: Witnessing Racial Violence in America, 1890–1940*. Chapel Hill: University of North Carolina Press, 2009.

Woodruff, Nan Elizabeth. *American Congo: The African American Freedom Struggle in the Delta*. Cambridge: Harvard University Press, 2003.

Woods, Clyde Adrian. *Development Arrested: The Blues and Plantation Power in the Mississippi Delta*. New York: Verso, 1998.
Woolfolk, Margaret Elizabeth. *A History of Crittenden County, Arkansas*. Greenville, South Carolina: Southern Historical Press, 1991.
Wright, George C. *Racial Violence in Kentucky, 1865–1940: Lynchings, Mob Rule, and "Legal Lynchings."* Baton Rouge: Louisiana State University Press, 1990.
Wright, John D., Jr. "Lexington's Suppression of the 1920 Will Lockett Lynch Mob." *Register of the Kentucky Historical Society* 84 (1986): 263–279.
Wright, Richard. *Richard Wright: Later Works: Black Boy (American Hunger), The Outsider*. New York: Library of America, 1991.
Uncle Tom's Children. New York: Harper Collins, 2008.
Wright Austin, Sharon D. *The Transformation of Plantation Politics: Black Politics, Concentrated Poverty, and Social Capital in the Mississippi Delta*. Albany: State University of New York Press, 2006.
Zangrando, Robert L. *The NAACP Crusade against Lynching, 1909–1950*. Philadelphia: Temple University Press, 1980.
Ziglar, William. "'Community on Trial': The Coatesville Lynching of 1911." *Pennsylvania Magazine of History and Biography* 106 (1982): 245–270.
"The Decline of Lynching in America." *International Social Science Review* 63 (1988): 14–25.

Index

For EU product safety concerns, contact us at Calle de José Abascal, 56–1°, 28003 Madrid, Spain or eugpsr@cambridge.org.

www.ingramcontent.com/pod-product-compliance
Ingram Content Group UK Ltd.
Pitfield, Milton Keynes, MK11 3LW, UK
UKHW022125080726
473066UK00009B/364

* 9 7 8 1 1 0 7 6 2 0 3 7 7 *